ON GARDEN STYLE

Bunny Williams

with Nancy Drew

ON GARDEN STYLE

SIMON &
SCHUSTER
EDITIONS

A Seth Godin Production

SIMON & SCHUSTER EDITIONS
Rockefeller Center
1230 Avenue of the Americas
New York, New York 10020

SIMON & SCHUSTER EDITIONS
and colophon are trademarks of
Simon & Schuster Inc.

Designer:
Rebecca Rose, Vignelli Associates
Illustrator:
David Connell
Photo editor:
Alexandra Truitt

Manufactured in the
United States of America
10 9 8 7 6 5 4 3 2 1

Library of Congress
Cataloging-in-Publication Data
Williams, Bunny, date.
On garden style / Bunny Williams with
Nancy Drew.
p. cm.
Includes bibliographical references
and index.
1. Gardening. 2. Plants, Ornamental.
3. Gardens—Styles. 4. Garden structures.
I. Drew, Nancy, date. II. Title.
SB453.W493 1998   97-41699
712'.6—dc21   CIP

ISBN 0-684-82605-4

*Frontispiece: The only flat, open, sunny
space on my property in Falls Village,
Connecticut, became what I call the "formal
garden," one enclosed by a hemlock hedge
on one side and a stone wall opposite.
The columns of lattice were placed to create
a room within a room and to give me
more spaces for planting. The sequence of
openings from the two large pots of plumbagos
through the low box hedge to the lattice
arbor framed by the old apple trees beckons
you to wander through.*

TEXT CREDITS

Excerpt from "La Figlia che Piange," in
Collected Poems 1909–1962 by T. S. Eliot.
Copyright © 1936 by Harcourt Brace &
Company. Copyright © 1964, 1963 by
T. S. Eliot, reprinted by permission of
the publisher.

"The Place," from *New and Selected Poems
1923–1985* by Robert Penn Warren.
Copyright © 1985 by Robert Penn Warren.
Reprinted by permission of Random
House, Inc.

"The Red Wheelbarrow" by William
Carlos Williams, from *Collected Poems
1909–1939, Volume I.* Copyright © 1938 by
New Directions Publishing Corp.
Reprinted by permission of New
Directions Publishing Corp.

"Atmosphere—Inscription for a Garden
Wall," from *The Poetry of Robert Frost,*
edited by Edward Connery Lathem.
Copyright © 1956 by Robert Frost.
Copyright © 1928 by Henry Holt & Co.,
Inc., © 1969 by Henry Holt & Co., Inc.
Reprinted by permission of Henry Holt
& Co., Inc.

Excerpt from *The Stones of Florence* by Mary
McCarthy, reprinted by permission of
Harcourt, Brace & Company.

Excerpt from *A History of Gardens and
Gardening* by Edward Hyams. Published
in the U.S.A. in 1971 by Praeger
Publishers, Inc. Copyright © text Mrs.
Mary Patricia Bacon 1971. Reproduced
with permission of Greenwood Publishing
Group, Inc., Westport, CT.

"Lilacs" from *The Complete Poetical Works
of Amy Lowell.* Copyright © 1955 by
Houghton Mifflin Company, © renewed
1983 by Houghton Mifflin Company,
Brinton P. Roberts, and G. D'Andelot
Belin, Esq. Previously published in *What's
O'Clock.* Reprinted by permission of
Houghton Mifflin Co. All rights reserved.

ACKNOWLEDGMENTS

It is to gardeners of great vision and style that we must turn to expand and grow. Among them are the following, into whose gardens I have ventured to take the reader: Bill Blass, Robert Dash, James David, Oscar de la Renta, Ken Druse, Ryan Gainey, Billy Goldsmith, Albert Hadley, Med Lange, Jack Lenor Larsen, Elise Lufkin, Dick Martin, Steve Martino, Nancy McCabe, Charlotte Peters and Daniel Ward, Nancy Power, Dean Riddle, Marco Polo Stufano, Laura and Rick Talaske, Michael Trapp, Oehme van Sweden, and Jaques Wirtz.

Anyone who knows me well knows that one thing I can do is talk—but write, that is another thing. So, to Nancy Drew, who captured my voice from millions of miles of tapes, I give heartfelt thanks. To Lisa DiMona, Seth Godin, Constance Herndon, and Alexandra Truitt for their continuous support and encouragement. To David Connell for the marvelous artwork that ornaments the book. And to Rebecca Rose for capturing a vision and then improving it for the design of the book.

In addition to the wonderful people who opened their gardens to us, I also wish to thank the many others who contributed their enthusiasm, time, and expertise to this project: Anne Cusack, Cathie Denckla, Kathleen Drew, Phil Eichler, Joan Gertz and Mike McCabe, Peter Joel Harrison, Polly Hawkins, Michael Hoffman, Bob Hursthouse, Lois and Gerald Johnson, Gary Jones, Hannah Kime, Scott Kunst, Charlotte Lyons, Mimi McBride, Tony Milburn, Gretta Moorhead, Phil Mumford, Debbie Munson, May Nakib, Nasser Nakib, Sally Paul, Anita Philipsborn, Frank Pollina, Kathryn Quinn, Karen Redford, Cec and Bruce Reinwald, Jim Rutledge, Donna Schwake, Ellen Todd, and Cheryl Vander Weit.

BUNNY WILLIAMS

In addition to those Bunny has already thanked above, I would like to give special thanks to my family, Kevin, Ben, and Harry Horan, for their love and good cheer during the writing of this book; to Beth Austin for whimsical poems and welcome critiques; to Colleen Berk and Alex Kotlowitz for their unfailing encouragement; and especially to Bunny, who taught me to see gardens through new eyes.

NANCY DREW

*To John, for his constant support and encouragement,
and to Debbie Munson, who has helped me nurture my garden
from its beginning.*

Contents

IMAGINE

Chapter One:
One Gardener's Journey

As far back as my memory takes me, I have been smitten by gardens. I grew up in the rolling countryside of Virginia, where I spent my summers tagging after my mother through beds of flowers and endless rows of tomatoes and cabbages. Often it was my job to pick whatever was ripe, and that is the memory that stays with me now. It's a warm summer afternoon, the light is golden, the birds are chirping, and I'm out there happily picking peas for dinner.

For some people the scent of a rose or a lilac jogs fond memories of childhood moments in a garden. For me, it is the crunch of a raw pea, fresh from its pod.

The career I chose as a young woman placed me firmly indoors, far afield from that country garden. I landed my dream job as an apprentice with the New York interior design firm of Parish-Hadley. I loved the easy, comfortable, but stylish interiors that defined the Parish-Hadley look. One spring in those early years at the firm, the memory of my parents' garden took up residence in my mind and wouldn't go away. I was a newlywed then, living in a cramped apartment. As I looked out at a landscape of rooftops and trees caged in wrought iron, I desperately longed for a green space of my own.

My First Garden

On a visit to see friends in Connecticut's northwest corner, my husband and I found a tiny weekend cottage out in the middle of a vast green field. As soon as we rented the place from the charming English couple who owned it, we mowed a lawn and set about making a garden.

I knew almost nothing about gardens. I could identify a

I don't know how many times I was taken by my parents to this garden at Morven in Charlottesville, Virginia, but it certainly made a lasting impression. The rooms created by the surrounding boxwood hedge are softened in a marvelous way by the lovely flower beds placed in an open field.

lily and a petunia, but that was about it. I studied a Wayside Gardens catalog, which offered three flower bed diagrams—A, B, or C—and decided that was for me. Hurriedly, I ordered up A and B, while my poor husband double-dug a space out in the middle of the yard. When the cardboard boxes arrived, we opened them like Christmas presents. We put in the little plants, sat back, and waited.

The flowers sprang up as if in a cartoon—I swear, the lilies were ten feet tall. The elderly English couple, who *knew* gardening, were astonished, and word spread rapidly among neighbors, who came over to gape at the flowers and congratulate us. Only later did we learn our garden was positioned on a former cow pasture.

That first garden had little to do with the color of our thumbs but it was great fun, and to this day I have never grown such luxuriant flowers. Nevertheless, by the end of August, I knew something was missing.

In Search of Atmosphere

What the garden lacked, of course, was structure. These were plants plunked down in the middle of the lawn without any rhyme or reason. Our little plot did qualify as a garden—the foxgloves grew, and I had wonderful bouquets each weekend for the house—but it was not beautiful. The plot had no relation to the house, no shape, no backdrop. And clearly no style.

By the following summer, I was humbled but a bit wiser. I made a vegetable garden, this time with a path and an inexpensive but serviceable wood fence enclosing it. That path and collection of boards were all it took to get the message across to me: Structure counts. Structure not only enhances a garden, it *is* a garden as much as anything you plant within it.

Learning Lessons

Those two early gardens marked the beginning of a learning process that continues to this day. I have studied garden design and plants over the ensuing years to discover how they conspire to give a garden atmosphere. Because the best part of a garden, for me, is being *in* it. And the most magical gardens, those that evoke the strongest emotion, are a combination of solid structure, wonderful plants, and delightful garden ornaments.

Ten years ago I bought an old Federal-style house in that same corner of Connecticut and set out in earnest to apply what I had learned in the intervening years to several new gardens. Here I have found that the lessons I've learned as an interior designer are inseparably woven into my gardening style. The issues I grapple with every day in working with clients—scale, texture, color, and use of space—present themselves each weekend in my garden. My work background has been an invaluable resource in making the "rooms" that constitute my Connecticut garden.

A few years later, in 1991, I opened a garden store on New York's Upper East Side with my dear friend and partner, John Rosselli, an antique dealer who not only has a wonderful eye for objects with history and character, but an uncanny knack for growing things, too. Treillage (French for "trellis work") is the natural outcome of the gardening

*A glimpse inside Treillage shows a world of possibility for
structural elements and ornament in a garden—everything from
statuary, wooden obelisks, and chairs for outdoor rooms to
rustic Tuscan olive jars and formal French urns.*

Artist unknown (Iranian), Bagh-i-Wafa, Emperor Babur Directs His Gardeners While Envoys Wait, Jelalabad, c. 1519. Victoria and Albert Museum, London.

The garden has been a sanctuary from its very beginning. This sixteenth-century Persian miniature shows a paradise that is created within walls in contrast to the disorder and chaos of the outside. In a way, this contrast is what we want to achieve in our own gardens.

journeys both John and I have traveled. There we have the pleasure of expressing our viewpoints with the objects we present to other gardeners.

I am a self-educated gardener, as most of us are. In the twenty-some years since I made my first little garden, it has been a constant source of pleasure to curl up with garden books, to visit public gardens around the world, to seek out-of-the-way private gardens, and to learn from the people who create and maintain both great and small ones.

I have been especially blessed to have two extraordinary garden designers as friends, Nancy Goslee Power and Nancy McCabe, as well as many other friends—devoted amateurs like myself—who have shared books, catalogs, ideas, plants, and travel in pursuit of gardening knowledge.

RETHINKING GARDENING

At a bookstore recently, while perusing shelf after shelf of gardening selections, I asked myself, "Who in her right mind would want to write another gardening book?" But I realized that many of those books address horticulture, while few communicate the importance of a garden's whole design.

In this book, I'm asking you to reframe the popular notion, held by many Americans, of what a garden is. Too often a perennial border is equated with a garden; that's comparable to mistaking a couch for a room. I'm asking you to think about the room first, and then decide how you will furnish it.

More than ever we want to connect intimately with nature, to make for ourselves private green places of beauty and serenity. But serenity is hard to come by if you embark upon a labor-intensive plan that requires far more of you than you're able to give. Many a novice has been stopped in her tracks by flower catalogs advising her on color progression and compatibility, when in fact she may just have time to water a few pots. It's important, in seeking your own sanctuary, to define gardening in a way that works for you.

By redefining "garden" to include simple but tranquil schemes—a high green hedge with a mossy stone floor, plus a bench for sitting, and just one ornamental focal point, perhaps a fountain or beautifully pruned tree—the dream becomes attainable. Add flowers if you will, but they're not required in order to have a garden.

In my own explorations, I've found that some of the most comforting sanctuaries are simple, with limited plant material. *And the structural elements of those gardens—the cool arbor, the rustic path—contribute as much to soothing the soul of the visitor as the most elaborately planted beds and borders.*

STRUCTURE AND DETAIL

This book is about the elements that make stylish gardens everywhere: the structural "bones" that hold together the garden and the details that, layer by layer, create mood and character. It is a guide based on my own gardening journey, and a sourcebook for nonprofessional gardeners who want to create that intangible delight—atmosphere— in their own backyards.

By the way, you won't find much advice here on floral picture-making: that is, which perennials look fabulous together. There are many other sources for that type of information, provided by experts. What I can share with other gardeners is a *way of seeing* that helps you look beyond the obvious things you take for granted, and to compose garden rooms with excitement and feeling.

Garden magic results when a gardener has a clear view of the big picture and a mastery of detail. It comes from consciously examining every aspect of your garden, from the bricks chosen for the front path to the way in which you store your gardening tools.

The Big Picture: Structure
Gardens, like fashion models, can wear any style if they have good "bones." Its bones give a garden form and remain the same throughout the seasons. They are made of hardscape materials—the well-conceived stone walk, the circular concrete pond, the vine-supporting wooden pergola—and of living plants such as hedges, or trees placed in the parallel lines of an *allée,* or grass covering a bowl shaped from the earth. Alive or not, these bones are the garden's permanent foundation pieces. Overgrown with summer foliage or sculpturally naked in winter, they make graphic statements in the landscape.

Structure also refers to the architectural form of the plant itself—the tall arborvitae that works almost as an outdoor column, the clump of a white birch that stands vaselike against a green hedge, the graphic form of an aloe plant.

Underpinning great gardens everywhere are good bones. Without them, you'll end up with merely a collection of plants, as I did in my first garden.

Mood: Small Details Create Atmosphere
Once the bones of your garden are in place, you can dress them in any number of ways. When I do interior spaces, I have to be certain the floor plan's structure is right first or I will forever be fighting its flaws. But the decisions I make to furnish the room are what really set the mood, whether the room is going to have country pine furniture or an eighteenth-century Louis XVI commode with ormolu mounts. Those choices range from the sublime—choosing a supple velvet for drapes—to the mundane, such as where to place a light switch. Every one of those decisions affects the atmosphere of that room.

The same can be said of gardens. Many small style choices add up to *mood.* And in garden sanctuaries, as in other artistic endeavors, God is in the details. When you understand the mood you're after in your garden, you'll know how to dress it. Making appropriate choices for path, fence, and terrace materials becomes easier, and editing out the inappropriate stuff is also easier.

Gardens are sensual experiences that require the same attention to detail you lavish on a beautiful interior room. If the color of your watering hose is visually jarring, it can undo the magic in a wink. That's why detail counts.

THE OUTDOOR ROOM—
A WAY TO THINK ABOUT THE GARDEN
With centuries of great garden design to guide us, why are so many of us overwhelmed by the prospect of designing a garden? Why are we game to decorate interior rooms, but utterly flummoxed by the challenge of designing the piece

LIGUSTRUM HEDGE

PERGOLA

ALLÉE OF TREES

Guisto Utens, Villa Castello, 1599, Museo di Firenza com'era, Florence.

While most of us don't have homes like the Medicis' Villa Castello, designed in the sixteenth century by Niccolo Tribolo, we can take lessons from its classic structure. The separate gardens have their own identities but are all linked by axial organization to each other and to the house—an idea we can carry over on a smaller scale in our own homes and gardens.

CYPRESS

17

This "garden in the woods" in Norfolk is typical of the kind of Virginia garden that I grew up with. The open structure and fenced garden enhance the natural beauty of the woods in a particularly nice way and give us a place to linger and enjoy the dogwood in spring.

By gardens, naturally, I do not mean places to grow flowers, but landscapes that have form and incident much as a great interior space must have form and incident. As a highboy gives emphasis to a gracious Colonial room so a gazebo gives focus and meaning to an outside "room." "Gardens" in this sense are more important, bigger, more meaningful as works of architecture than even the greatest interior spaces.

Philip Johnson, *Philip Johnson: The Glass House*, 1993[1]

of earth behind the house? I think it may be as simple as this: The sky is so big, the horizon so far. Without the parameters of walls, floor, and ceiling, we give up before we begin. But by thinking of the garden in architectural terms, we go a long way toward demystifying its design.

Enclosure, more than any other aspect, separates the garden room from the great outdoors. The very qualities we seek in our homes—privacy, serenity, and intimacy—can be approached in nature by creating "walls." A garden room is somehow set apart from the rest of the outdoors, whether by a fence, a stone wall, a hedge or trees. You have the sense of being in a circumscribed space. But there's more to making a wonderful room than simply erecting walls.

To create an outdoor room, you have to grapple with the same issues you face in designing an interior space. How do you enter the room? How does the room relate to others? Where are windows and doorways located, and what views do these openings frame? What detail—plants, furniture, and ornaments—do you furnish it with to express your personal style? Will the overall design you choose be formal or informal? What mood are you after?

Garden rooms allow you to create intimacy where there is none. They allow you to block out a bad view, or focus the eye when you have a glorious view that competes with your garden. They permit a sense of discovery and surprise. And they allow two gardeners in one household (or one rather schizophrenic gardener such as myself) to have several distinctly different gardens on one property that are connected by the "hallway" of a path. And, interestingly enough, by breaking up a property into several rooms, you

achieve the illusion of having more rather than less space.

Not all open landscapes call for garden rooms, of course. Meadows of wildflowers and orchards, for example, are gardens that require no walls. And some people might find the idea of enclosure too claustrophobic. It's all a matter of taste and feel.

I recall the first time I visited a new client's home that was built with almost no interior walls—in essence it was one big room. When I opened the front door I could see everything—living room, kitchen, dining room, library. I felt strangely uncomfortable, and I knew it was because there was no mystery in that house. I want to be drawn to walk farther into the space and have it *unfold* to me as I go. I feel the same way about gardens. Not everyone does, I realize. But if you enjoy a bit of intrigue as I do, the approach will soon make sense.

The "outdoor room" is a handy metaphor for an interior designer, I admit, but in one way or another, outdoor rooms have existed in different cultures throughout history. The lovely muraled interior gardens of Pompeii, preserved by Vesuvius's eruption in the first century A.D., reveal a people who so valued their roses, pear and fig trees, and mosaic garden fountains that they built their homes around them.[2]

At the heart of the garden room is our impulse, as human beings, to live out-of-doors as much as we can. Like other gardeners from different times, you can create rooms that offer the comforts and privacy of shelter with the delights of growing flowers and food, eating and playing out in the open air. Some tastes don't alter much in the course of a thousand years.

Chapter Two: Getting Started

Where do we begin to make enchanting garden rooms? My first garden taught me only too well that ordering up a load of perennials is not the answer. Great gardens begin in our own hearts and minds, and on our own properties. They are shaped by our memories and the landscape and climate in which we live.

Before you put pencil to paper, it's important to start with some basic understandings. You must find what you truly love and want in a garden, and you must understand the strengths and weaknesses of your property. You also have to realistically assess how much time you can give to maintaining a garden. Once you've merged your "givens" with your heart's desire into a workable vision, you'll be ready to sketch out the floor plan and furnish its rooms with the sights and sounds and smells that say "garden" to you. The process is a longer route than a quick trip to the nursery, but well worth the time.

The Givens

Every gardener has been dealt a hand before he even touches a spade. These are the givens—the soil, the climate, light and shade, the flavor of the community, the topography of the region. Add in the slice of the land you call your own and the house sitting on it, and you've got a snapshot of the parameters within which you have to work.

In any scenario, your challenge is to meld those elements into a unified whole. To connect the house to the land with a garden. To make something beautiful out of what you have been given. To leave your imprint on the land. That's what style is all about.

Louvered doors placed in a wall made of columns and lattice panels shield the parking area from view in Michael Trapp's garden. Interestingly, all of the structural elements in this garden are made from recycled materials.

Understanding
What You Have

A Questionnaire

You may live in a river-town shingle cottage next to a bluff, surrounded by soaring old maple trees. You may inhabit a new French Provincial house set out in a former cow pasture with nary a tree in sight. Maybe, behind your suburban ranch house, you have a pie-shaped wedge of grass that slopes down five feet from one side to the other. Possibly the concrete rectangle behind your brick rowhouse gets almost no sun.

Some books recommend that you begin planning a garden with graph paper. This is not one of them. Instead, find a quiet time and come outside.

Public Spaces—The Front

Most of us live in communities where the front of the property tends to be a more public, formal space and the back is more private. To get an overview, walk far enough away from your home to take in the house, lot, and close neighboring homes in one view.

What style is your house? Is it traditional or modern? A brick Georgian, perhaps, or wood ranch house? Or is it a mix of many styles? Note all the different building materials in the house. In planning a new garden, you want to create a feeling that is consistent with the mood and style of your home. That's not to say you will create a historically accurate knot garden for your Tudor house, but you will want some continuity of feeling.

Many of today's newer houses are a blend of architectural styles; most, though, lean in the direction of either traditional or modern. Look to the lines of the house and

BOXWOOD HEDGE

the materials in it for cues on how to hardscape your property. If the house incorporates stone, a stone path will be appropriate.

Though your gardening energies will more likely go into your private garden, every effort should be made to give the front an attractive design. The planting and pathway may be quite simple, but should pull you toward the front door with visually appealing elements, such as a low boxwood hedge or rows of nepeta along the path.

Is the foundation planting overgrown or inappropriate? Foundation plantings became popular in this century as a way to conceal raised foundations. But they're often grown far beyond the original planter's expectations by the time we inherit them. If you have scraggly evergreens or giant spruces dwarfing and obscuring the house, it's time to make some difficult choices. Do you even need foundation plantings? Don't be afraid to edit; it's often the better part of landscaping an older home. That goes for trees and shrubs away from the house, too. If they're in the wrong place, they may be real stumbling blocks to making a plan that works.

Examine how you enter your house. Does the walkway go directly from street to front door, or does it meander? Is it made of materials consistent with the appearance of your house? I prefer to have a straight and direct path from street or front parking area to my door. This is a personal preference, though. If you like a curving path, make sure it doesn't meander too much. Your mailman will thank you.

PARKING

How do you move from car to house? Study your driveway — it's a large mass in any home landscape. If it's supposed to be straight, is it? If it curves, is it a weak curve? If it's blacktop, would it look much better if concrete pavers, tumbled to look aged, were used? Is there a turnaround? Are parked cars visible in your driveway from your garden? Great expanses of driveway can detract from the view of your house. I have a long asphalt driveway leading from the main road to my house in the country. A top layer of gravel (called armor coating) has been worked into the asphalt to soften the color of the drive and to keep it from looking like a stretch of highway.

Also critical is where you park your automobiles. I hate looking at cars from my garden and feel it's essential to screen them from view. If the focus of your house is to the back or side, the front is a great place to park; however, if your terrace is on the front of your home, you'll want to park in the back or on the side. If you must park in sight of your garden, block out the parking area with high shrubs or a tall fence or lattice screen.

Also note the garage. Many an American house has a two-car garage attached to it that is nearly as big as the house itself. How do you soften it to make it a less blatant feature? Ideally, when you build a new house you will put the garage doors to the side or back of the structure so that the attached garage appears to be a room of the house itself. If you already own a house with an attached garage, imagine how it might be softened with vines, perhaps, or large container plantings on each side of the doors. Or cut out a planting area on

VINES AROUND GARAGE DOORS

each side and grow euonymus, privet, or pyracantha around each door. Clip it to form a frame.

THE LAY OF THE LAND
Is there an elephant buried in your front yard? That's how Midwest landscaper Bob Hursthouse describes the berms rising like bumps in front of new suburban homes that sit on the otherwise flat prairie. Level that berm if it doesn't look natural. Prairies are flat; so are painters' canvases. Make something beautiful on that flat surface.

How does your present landscaping relate to that of the houses adjoining yours? In planned communities everywhere, from city lots to suburban cul-de-sacs, the front of the property often shares a consistent look with adjoining properties. Some of the most beautiful areas in this country are neighborhoods where trees were planted when the streets were laid out by planners, often around the turn of the century. Rows of trees may line the streets, creating arching *allées* that everyone enjoys and from which everyone benefits. By keeping the front plantings of properties roughly consistent, grand vistas are sometimes created that give the homes in that community a sense of unity.

You don't have to plant grass like everyone else on the block, but you might consider a low-growing ground cover such as ivy or periwinkle instead of a tall stand of prairie grasses out by the street curb. In a vista of scattered trees and unenclosed green undergrowth, think twice before you erect a bright white arbor and picket fence. Respect shared views and save those contrary impulses for your private garden, where it's fair game to pursue any theme you want. When significant space separates houses, you have more latitude to pursue a scheme that relates only to your house.

How does your current landscaping relate to the broader community? If your property is part of a housing development established in the last hundred years, it undoubtedly bears little resemblance to the original landscape. A northern Illinois suburb planned on a grid at the turn of the century, for example, reveals few clues that at one time the land was a sea of grasses and wildflowers punctuated by bur oaks.

Still, it is essential to understand the native inclinations of soil and plant life. It keeps you from pursuing an impossible dream—an English-style flower garden in the desert, for example. I am not a purist who believes that only native plant material should be used in a garden or that all gardens in one area of the country should look alike. But I do believe in growing what's happy in my part of the world.

There is a feeling to every geographic area that suggests certain choices in plants and stone. One of the main motivations for creating a garden is to feel connected to the land. On my own property, I don't want to live as people did in the eighteenth century, but I do want to remain sensitive to the history of this area. In a farm community covered with dry walls of native field stone, it felt right to add such a wall to my own land. The wall continues a New England tradition and connects me to the history of this place.

Top left: Vibrant color is at home in the bright light of Austin, Texas.

Above left: A mix of color—in the stone, adobe, and wooden door—makes for great style.

Top right: Architectural plants enhance the entrance of a Santa Monica, California, home. Aloes underplanted with succulents provide dramatic form and texture near the simple stucco home, and the placement of the wooden gate within the high privacy wall invites you to enter.

Above right: Created by Elise Lufkin and set against the greenhouse that leads to her back door, this Connecticut garden is also beautiful in winter, when only the form is visible. Brick from the house was carried over to the garden path.

25

A View of the Garden

Now walk through your house toward the private area where you will garden. First, though, observe the views you have of the garden area from your windows and doorways. So much of designing is picture-making. The window and door act as frames for your view of the garden. Ideally, something wonderful — a beautifully pruned tree, an inviting path, a display of perennials, a fountain or arbor—is centered in those openings.

Private Spaces—The Back or Side Garden

Begin assessing your private garden space by starting with the outdoor living area closest to your house. Walk the perimeter of your ideal terrace or loggia, keeping in mind its proportion in relation to the house. Inside that area, place a chair where you would most want to sit. Does an existing enclosure offer you privacy or do you feel exposed? Which is more appropriate to the architecture of your house, an elevated living area or one at ground level? What materials are used in your house that might be used in a terrace? Also, how is the view from where you sit? Is it a terrific view of the mountains or ocean? Or do you have a terrific view of your neighbor's permanently parked cabin cruiser? If you have a pretty view, imagine how you might frame it. Perhaps you can borrow a view of a neighbor's lovely garden with some imaginative pruning. Imagine how you might screen out an ugly view.

The Terrace

Look at how your house connects with the earth. If you currently have steps but lack a terrace, does the house appear grounded to its site? If you do have a terrace near the house, is it located close enough to the kitchen for serving outdoor meals? Is there room for a table and four or six chairs, plus room to maneuver? (This requires roughly ten by twelve feet.) What is the most direct path from stove and counter to outside eating area? Note where your grill is located and whether it's an eyesore.

Other Rooms

Look out at your property from where you sit and think about how you want to use the garden. Does a sunny area suggest a spot for a kitchen garden? A swimming pool? Where would you put a service area to hide all your garden "stuff," from hibachis to shovels and rakes? Where would you locate a potting shed?

Light and Shade

Observe light and shade in your garden. Is it heavy or dappled shade? Partial or full sunlight? Intensely bright light most of the day or misty and filtered light? Understanding your light will take some time if you haven't observed it closely in the past. It's important to watch how it changes through the day and through the seasons. That's why, if you've recently purchased a home, it's advisable before you plan a new garden to go through one whole year's cycle. See where the sun falls in the afternoons and what springs up next to the house before you tear into the yard.

Do you have too much or too little tree canopy? Trees take the place of a ceiling in a garden, regulating the light and contributing to the intimacy and sense of closure you find in memorable places. Trees can be chosen for color, form, function, or purely emotional reasons. I find few pleasures sweeter than lying on the ground in fall and looking up at my maple's golden branches framing the blue sky.

OTHER BACKGROUND CONSIDERATIONS

What are the other givens in your private space? Observe in the private garden the things you looked at in front: the lay of the land, the current plantings, the views of any parked cars.

Now walk to the far end of your lot. If you enter through a gate, either at the back or side of your garden, what kind of gate would look good? An old salvaged antique iron one, placed between brick columns and set into a high hedge? Or perhaps a new gate fashioned by a local sculptor? Look back at the house. Is there a spot near your back gate for a sitting area that would permit a view of the house and another perspective on the garden? Sometimes we miss the most pleasant views by only looking out from the house.

Having walked your property, stand back and take another long look. Is there some theme or element in the land itself that suggests a direction for your garden? In *The Education of a Gardener*, the great English landscape designer Russell Page suggests taking design clues from existing features of your property, such as the "shape of a tree or a group of trees, [or] a change in level."[1] Such existing features can serve as starting points that inspire a design. For example, a magnificent old horse chestnut tree that blocks the sun in most of your yard may not only suggest a shady hosta garden as a theme but may also serve as a focal point in the design of that hosta garden.

Given an open piece of land with few trees, Belgian landscape designer Jacques Wirtz created a magical garden at Hazelet in Belgium. The combination of simple elements —hedges, paths, and water —is not only beautiful, but serene.

TAKING CUES FROM NATURE

Since the eighteenth century, when some English gardeners turned their backs on the rigid and formal style of the times toward a more natural parklike landscape, garden writers have echoed poet/philosopher Alexander Pope's advice to look to nature for cues in how to design one's landscape.

In large properties, consulting the genius of the place means simply respecting and enhancing what's already there when planning your garden. If you are fortunate to live in a woodland or near a stream, a meadow, or rock outcroppings, take your cues from those features. If you live on a sand dune, respect its genius by responding to its contours and native plant material.

If you live in a typical suburb, though, and head out to the backyard to follow Pope's advice, you may conclude that the genius of your particular place has flown the coop. In fact, just *looking* at the yard may make you feel mean.

Those of us who garden on a small scale in flat rectangles or pie-shaped wedges, in subdivisions where the flavor of the original landscape has long been lost, must use our own wits to create some gardening brilliance. In the absence of the land's strong features guiding us in a specific direction, we have to create our own "incidents" and our own views rather than respond to picturesque features that nature has already endowed.

The simple act of enclosing your space sets you in that direction. Enclosure permits an intimate garden world that can be furnished with any number of wonders, and soon the lack of a stream or sweeping view becomes unimportant.

Within that enclosed space, though, you can tap the hidden genius of the soil and climate. To understand the possibilities, study your soil and what grows in it. Get in your car and drive around your community. Brake for thriving trees and shrubs and wildflowers. Visit a local arboretum or botanic garden. Take inspiration from a stand of oaks surrounded by a mass of bluebells. If they grow so beautifully in that spot, it's likely they'll do so in your own yard. You may just have one oak tree set into a blue carpet, but that's all it takes.

TAKING CUES FROM HOME

The other place to look for design cues is your own house. In our small American gardens, the landscaping must respond to the house in some way; proximity demands it. Look to the style of your home for direction. It will help you rule out designs that are wrong from the beginning. My Colonial-style New England garden, for example, planted with traditional flowers and layered with the small details I love, would be entirely inappropriate next to a modern house set in the arid climate of Los Angeles.

Since everyone needs a place to sit and view the garden, and since a terrace works as a transition from house to nature, that may be the first room you plan. The rest of the garden rooms can evolve from that point, becoming perhaps less formal as you proceed away from the house into wilder gardens. By using materials compatible with those in the house and by keeping the mood of the garden rooms close to the home consistent with the house, you can pretty much guarantee success in making appropriate

To build, to plant, whatever you intend,
To rear the Column or the Arch to bend,
To swell the Terras, or to sink the Grot;
In all, let Nature never be forgot . . .
Consult the Genius of the Place in all;
That tells the Waters or to rise, or fall . . .

Alexander Pope, *Epistle IV: To Richard Boyle, Earl of Burlington*, 1731[2]

The dry earth was ticking under the sun
and the crickets rasped.
"It's real godforsaken country," said Louis.
"Makes me feel mean," said Adam.

John Steinbeck, *East of Eden*, 1952[3]

choices for your property. That doesn't mean you have to slavishly re-create a French garden for your French Provincial house, though.

Consider the fifty-by-fifty-foot Connecticut garden of the great interior designer Albert Hadley. His house is an Italianate Victorian stationmaster's home, but his taste in gardens does not run to flower beds, as the original owner's might have. Instead, he wanted a cool green outdoor room, with only occasional touches of color.

The design he settled on is a simple fountain and circular pool surround by bluestone and set into a square of English ivy, each corner of which is marked by a stone ball finial. Albert Hadley's geometrical green room is pure elegance and pure simplicity, and, in the spirit of formal French and Italian gardens, responds in proportion and formality to the house's lines. But he has kept the plantings soft rather than rigid by using ivy and old-fashioned shrubs, just the sort of plants one might have found in a Victorian garden. The resulting marriage of house and garden is seamless.

I think one buys a certain kind of house, most of the time, because something in the heart responds to it. We choose a rambling old farmhouse or a one-story modern house because they reflect how we think we want to live. So continuing the feeling of the house out into the garden should come naturally. If you've chosen a very modern house, it makes sense to treat the outside in a pared-down, sculptural, contemporary way. And if you've bought a cottage? There is, undoubtedly, someplace in your heart where a cottage garden resides, and you will garland your home with vines and plant its gardens exuberantly.

Interior designer Albert Hadley's Italian-inspired, all-green garden works beautifully next to his Victorian, Italianate house in Westport, Connecticut. The plan could have been inspired by one of the spaces from the lunette for the Medici villa on page 17.

It is worth any amount of effort to be able to see your house through the arch of a tree.

Thomas Church, *Gardens Are for People,* 1955[4]

Chapter Three: In Search of Personal Style

Adornment is never anything except a reflection of the heart.

Coco Chanel[1]

If you're not certain which garden style is right for you, go look in your closets. Is there more Chanel than Gap, more suits than jeans? Are there colorfully patterned vests and shirts that you layer on top of each other, or solid-colored pieces with simple lines that you wear unadorned, save for a bold piece of jewelry or a scarf?

Most people really do have defined personal styles, though they may think they don't. It's evident in the houses they choose and the way they furnish their rooms. Look at your own living quarters. Is the furniture precisely placed, or is there a looser, more scattered arrangement? Are the rooms filled cozily with clutter and collections, or are they spare and serene? Given the choice, would you buy a chrome and leather Barcelona chair, a mahogany Chippendale ladderback, a simple pine Shaker stool, or a brocade and fringed Victorian armchair? As a dream house, would you pick a Stickley Arts and Crafts bungalow, a modern box of glass and steel, a pink Art Deco Palm Beach villa, a rustic timber-beamed adobe hacienda? Your answers may help you understand what kind of garden you want.

There's not one "correct" approach, but you need to choose a direction to pursue in your garden. After you've had a look in your closet, look into your own heart. Your style will be an expression of what you find meaningful, what makes your heart sing.

Memory and Meaning

Gardens are as individual as fingerprints, especially when you include in them plants and objects that have meaning to you. Delve into your memories to find what you most love

I have always loved conservatories and kitchen gardens, so when I started working on my own garden, I combined these two areas. The conservatory was constructed of recycled windows and pilasters taken from a house on the Hudson River, and the kitchen garden adjoins it.

in a garden. Perhaps the fragrance of lilacs means "garden" to you because it takes you back to your mother's yard, for example. One male friend remembers being "neck high in roses" in his grandfather's Baltimore garden, and can't imagine his own without them. For me, a boxwood hedge will send me straight back to Charlottesville, Virginia, and seems somehow indispensable in my own garden.

Think of the spots you have visited, whether a friend's place or a quiet corner in a public garden, that gave you the kind of serenity you seek in your own space. Analyze what it was about that particular spot that made you feel good, then find ways to adapt that garden's mood to your own land.

It's important, I think, to find the cues that will comfort you in your own sanctuary, and to integrate them into the plan. Whether these cues are cuttings from the garden of a cherished friend, a tree planted at the birth of a child, or plants and ornaments that remind you of beautiful places you have visited, they make the garden distinctly your own.

PICTURE THIS

Picture how you want to *be* in your garden. Are you clipping cosmos from a cutting garden? Potting bulbs in a greenhouse? Sitting on a terrace chaise with the *New York Times* spread around you, along with pots of fragrant roses? Dining *alfresco* in a private woodland spot? The *kind* of garden you dream of will certainly propel you in a design direction. But there are many permutations of a flower garden, or even a vegetable garden. You still need to discover the mood and style you want.

You are the smells of all Summers . . .
The recollection of the gardens of little
children . . .

Amy Lowell, from "Lilacs"[2]

To help new clients identify their own personal styles, I always encourage them to bring magazine photos of rooms they love to our first meeting. Some clients are more prepared than others. A man might bring in only one photo and say, "I want that." Others have been collecting material for years. I recall a very dear client who showed up with two fat albums chock-full of clipped photos she had amassed over several years. I immediately saw a pattern emerge. She loved the look of a lived-in house, a mellow place with soft, faded colors and big comfortable rooms that look as if they have evolved over a long period of time. Other people will have cut out ten pictures of rooms that are serene, spare, modern, unfussy, and full of light. It is from these photos that I understand immediately the essence of what I have to accomplish.

You can begin a new garden in the same way, by collecting magazine photos of gardens that resonate in some way for you. Do you like the clean, precise, and orderly look of a formal garden? Or do you prefer a wilder, more overgrown, informal look? What the photos help you do is identify a mood and style to pursue, so that editing becomes easier.

FORMAL OR INFORMAL

Formal gardens are symmetrical and ordered; their geometric shapes, with straight lines and angles, are neat and precise. Trimmed hedges, topiary, and statues with classical themes are right at home in a formal garden.

Informal gardens have more fluid lines, more naturally arranged plantings. They are relaxed, looser, curvier, more

BIRD TOPIARY

ARCHITECTURAL TOPIARY

The Gardens of the Palace of Schönbrunn, *Canaletto, ca. 1750. Kunsthistorisches Museum, Vienna.*

Ultimate formal garden style is shown in this eighteenth-century painting, which depicts parterres, trees in pots, and rows of column topiary. The garden was created by the great architect J. B. Fischer von Erlach for the Austrian emperor Franz I.

CLIPPED HEDGE

After seeing the gardens of Majorelle House, the former studio of French painter Jacques Majorelle in Marrakesh, Morocco, I wanted to move to Florida, California, New Mexico, or Texas — anywhere that I could have the same marvelous colors and incredible plants.

This hillside of naturalized Chionodoxa sardensis *at Wave Hill in Riverdale, New York, is a perfect example of informal design at work in a wide-open space.*

mixed up. They often have an overgrown and abandoned feeling, expressing a greater sense of freedom than formal gardens. And the successful informal garden reveals little of the gardener's touch, while in fact it has often been managed as intensely as the formal garden.

"Formal" doesn't mean cold or stuffy, and "informal" doesn't mean unstructured. In fact, you can mix the two moods, as you would a Chippendale table with a straw basket. Formal geometric structure can be the essential organizer of the most wildly informal plantings, as it is in English gardens.

Some old notions about formal gardens need to be thrown out. While they have long been associated with traditional architecture, the fact is that formal garden geometry can look smashing with modern architecture. For what is "modern" but classic design stripped down to its bare essence? A modern American house could easily coexist with an Italian parterre garden because of its clean and simple lines. And what a wonderful opportunity to place a piece of contemporary sculpture in the same way a formal Italian garden might feature a classic statue.

Nor is formal gardening necessarily a higher maintenance proposition than an informal one. A hedge may have to be clipped twice a year, while an informal "natural" garden may require more weeding, fertilizing, and general attention.

Two gardens near my Connecticut home reveal the artistry that's possible in both formal and informal gardening. They have entirely different moods and inspirations, but both bear the marks of the garden artist: great design, wonderful plant material, and fantastic ornament.

Chauncy Stillman's all-green, formal garden, Wethersfield, is full of intimate rooms. Openings in hedges lead to new spaces and surprises, including this circular reflecting/swimming pool.

WETHERSFIELD

Chauncey Stillman's ten-acre garden, Wethersfield, is set atop a hill near Millbrook, New York, and overlooks some of the most beautiful rolling hills the East Coast has to offer. Stillman, a philanthropist, started making the gardens in the 1940s and continued over a twenty-five-year period to add to them. The owner chose the path that many a great gardener chooses who has fabulous views: He made a terrace for enjoying the vistas, then set apart his other gardens so that they do not compete with the countryside. Instead, he raised hedges to created formal gardens with atmosphere and focus of their own, yet with openings throughout for glimpses of the hills.

Italian in spirit, some of his garden rooms are tied to the Georgian-style house they adjoin. In one room, three "walls" of pleached beech trees adjoin a fourth, which is the brick wall of the house. In another room, the majestic twenty-foot-high deep green walls of an impeccably trimmed arborvitae hedge serenely encloses a space that is empty but for grass.

Elsewhere, paths and openings conspire to pull you farther into different rooms. A long tunnel of trained beech trees opens up into a view of a glistening white marble madonna against a red brick wall. A bower of purple wisteria arches over her head. Again and again, Stillman plays with your eye, closing up one space only to open another, and all the while achieving the most delicious sense of calm and sanctuary with stone and plants. The green architecture of Wethersfield, though suggestive of European garden formality, adapts itself beautifully to an American landscape.

INNISFREE

If Wethersfield is classically manicured, the two-hundred-acre preserve five miles away called Innisfree appears to have been untouched by the hand of man. No axis extending from the house exists here. Instead, Innisfree's builders, Walter and Marion Beck, took their inspiration in 1930 from a series of naturally enclosed gardens built by Wang Wei, an eighth-century Chinese painter and poet. The drawings of Wang Wei's natural enclosures reminded Walter Beck of the sides of a cup and inspired Innisfree's free-flowing yet self-contained landscapes, dubbed "cup gardens" by Beck.[3]

Innisfree gives the visitor the distinct sensation she has wandered into an enchanted painting. Its cup gardens are not technically rooms as Wethersfield's enclosed spaces are, yet they are framed by trees and stone outcroppings and reveal themselves as asymmetrical yet balanced vignettes.

In one spot, the earth has been contoured to make a semicircular berm that shelters a row of cleanly modern chairs. Nearby, six trees are arranged, shrinelike, around a tall, monolithic rock at their center. The pond makes another vignette, filled with irises and small islands sprouting neatly pruned willows.

There are no straight lines here. Nor are there statues. Instead, great boulders are treated as sculpture, set apart and sometimes set on end.

I love taking visitors to these two gardens in one day. The contrast is astounding, yet they are both at home in Dutchess County, New York, because they have been interpreted with native stone and plants well adapted to

At the Japanese-inspired Innisfree Garden in Millbrook, New York, simple wooden chairs are set under pollarded willow trees trained as giant parasols.

the area. And though inspired by European and Asian traditions, they are entirely American gardens.

Which way should you go, formal or informal? No one approach is right. What's important is that you choose a direction appropriate for your land, your home, and your own particular taste. If you have enough property and you love it all, you can have a little of both.

EXPOSURE: INSIGHTS FROM THE PAST, LESSONS FROM THE PRESENT

Who is born into this world a passionate collector of modern art or of fine antiques? No one. Personal style develops over time. If you feel you don't have a personal style, it's not because you lack imagination; more likely, you lack information. And for that dilemma I have one word: *exposure.*

Expose yourself to local private and botanical gardens, to books and magazine articles about garden style, and to the gardens of other cultures. Visit different kinds of gardens: woodland, prairie, desert, rock, knotted herb, kitchen, terrace, and others. Something will resonate for you.

Make America's historic gardens your vacation destinations. Visit early Colonial gardens at Williamsburg and Savannah; discover the historic California mission gardens at Carmel and Lompoc; wander the great estate gardens that are open to the public—Stan Hywet in Akron, Ohio; Naumkeag in Stockbridge, Massachusetts; and Bloedel Reserve on Bainbridge Island, Washington, among many others throughout the United States. (See the list in Gardener in Winter, page 250, for other suggestions.)

The idea of planting drifts of rhododendrons and azaleas among mature trees and leaving them to grow as they will is, after landscaping, the great English contribution to modern garden design.

Harold Nicolson, "Great Gardens," *New York Times Magazine,* 1963[4]

Exposure to a great garden's structure—whether it's an *allée* of lilacs underplanted with hostas at Long Island's Westbury Gardens or the stylish placement of one olive jar in a small, uncelebrated Italian garden—may spark an inspiration for an unforgettable element in your own home plot.

SOURCES OF INSPIRATION: OTHER CLIMATES, OTHER CULTURES

One of the most useful things you can do in exploring style possibilities is to study the gardens of countries with climates and terrain similar to your own. Garden designs in other cultures are a response to the environment in which they are made, and offer a wealth of ideas if your own climate and land are similar. If you live in Texas, I'm not recommending that you re-create Provence in your backyard, but you can pay attention to how southern French gardeners adapt their ideas to land much like yours.

The fortunate gardener who works the soil in Washington State shares a similar misty light and wet climate with the English gardener, for example. In southern coastal areas of the United States and in California, gardeners share the same concerns that Italian, other Mediterranean, and Mexican gardeners have: a need for shade and for cool breezes. And the age-old approaches— of vine-covered shelters and courtyards with cool fountains— make as much sense in Florida as they do in Spain.

Even if your climate differs from southern France or England, you can take design lessons from countries with distinctive styles. In the United States, our history of pleasure gardening is relatively young compared to that of

The Japanese, of course, are the great masters of using and defining what has been given. When I came back from Japan, I saw every rock in my meadow with fresh eyes, the whole state of New Hampshire as a vast Japanese rock garden, where the wildness, the casualness, is the quality to be preserved.

May Sarton, *Plant Dreaming Deep,* 1968[5]

many European and Asian cultures; they've had more time to refine garden design.

For example, French gardens teach us how to extend architecture into the landscape, relating home to earth with terraces and steps. The clean geometry of traditional French design, with its axial lines and symmetry, offers structural solutions for small American gardens. And the French *potager* is a model for anyone seeking to grow vegetables in a stylish way.

English gardeners are master plantspeople who often use neat geometrical underpinnings in their lush gardens, too. English gardening goddess Gertrude Jekyll elevated the herbaceous border to an art form, and Vita Sackville-West and Harold Nicolson at Sissinghurst, as well as Lawrence Johnston (a transplanted American) at Hidcote, left garden room legacies for anyone interested in learning how to make their own.

I've been charmed by the quiet intimacy of Portuguese gardens and the complicated geometry of Indian Mughal gardens. And Japanese gardens teach us the value of restraint and economy in small gardens, as well as the art of the pruner.

And Italian gardens? Perhaps no one makes a more persuasive argument for why Americans should look abroad for garden design inspiration than an American herself, Edith Wharton, in her 1904 book *Italian Villas and Their Gardens*. Her observations are as true today as they were then. Listen:

Though it is an exaggeration to say that there are no flowers in Italian gardens, yet to enjoy and appreciate the Italian garden-craft one must always bear in mind that it is independent of floriculture.

The Italian garden does not exist for its flowers; its flowers exist for it: they are a late and infrequent adjunct to its beauties, a parenthetical grace counting only as one more touch in the general effect of enchantment. This is no doubt partly explained by the difficulty of cultivating any but spring flowers in so hot and dry a climate, and the result has been a wonderful development of the more permanent effects to be obtained from the three other factors in garden-composition—marble, water and perennial verdure—and the achievement, by their skillful blending, of a charm independent of the seasons . . .

The garden-lover should not content himself with a vague enjoyment of old Italian gardens, but should try to extract from them principles which may be applied at home. He should observe, for instance, that the old Italian garden was meant to be lived in—a use to which, at least in America, the modern garden is seldom put. He should note that, to this end, the grounds were as carefully and conveniently planned as the house, with broad paths (in which two or more could go abreast) leading from one division to another; with shade easily accessible from the house, as well as a sunny sheltered walk for winter. . . . He should remember that the terraces and formal gardens adjoined the house, that the ilex or laurel walks beyond were clipped into shape to effect a transition between the straight lines of masonry and the untrimmed growth of the woodland to which they led, and that each step away from architecture was a nearer approach to nature.[6]

Roberto Burle Marx's own outdoor atelier in Rio de Janeiro is a perfect example of how strong planting and architecture can work in harmony. The cut stone path with a bed of rocks along its border, plus the extraordinary mixture of plants, create an exciting and modern entrance to the house.

Previous page: The formal tradition is beautifully illustrated in a great garden in Fiesole, Italy, called Gamberaia. Although this is a large garden, elements of it can be easily translated into a more modest scheme.

LOOKING TO THE FUTURE: ABSTRACT AND CONTEMPORARY

If Edith Wharton and Gertrude Jekyll offer us lessons from the past, Brazilian garden artist Roberto Burle Marx offers lessons specifically attuned to a modern audience. Marx, who began creating modernistic gardens in the 1930s, has been compared to Picasso for the artistic way he composed with plants. Not only did he paint abstract designs on the ground in living color, he also used plants as sculpture, combining them in unexpected ways.[7]

Marx particularly fascinates me, because I find myself more and more drawn to contemporary furniture and art. And while I will always love and own old things, I am excited by modernism, and in particular, the painterly abstractions that Marx and others have created with plants.

Contemporary houses call for a rethinking of traditional approaches to garden design. America has some extraordinary contemporary architects who are creating modern buildings, both private and public, that require landscaping with the same point of view. Add to modern architecture the facts of our hurried-up lives, and you can see the writing on the garden wall. We need gardens that are simple in design and equally simple to maintain.

And that's why mass planting, in the tradition of Marx, or the formal but simple hedge/stone/water gardens described by Edith Wharton can be both realistic and artfully beautiful. As we look to the future, I think many of us will choose cleaner and sparer gardens, with more naturalized plantings.

CHAPTER FOUR: PUTTING YOUR DREAMS TO WORK

Merging your dreams with your reality is tricky business. At the heart of making it happen is your success in defining gardening in a way that fits your life, space, and growing conditions. By accepting that the term "garden" doesn't have to mean Mr. du Pont's Winterthur, and by using plants that will succeed to create the effects you want, you can have your Eden and keep it, too, whether it's in a bog, a desert, or a cow pasture. When you accept the limitations you face, there's an odd sense of liberation. It frees you from impossible dreams and sets you on the way to creating something realistic and uniquely personal.

BUILDING GARDEN ROOMS — THE PROCESS

Getting from the dream stage to real garden rooms goes roughly like this. Once you have a good feel for your property and you've figured out how you will use different areas, begin with a sketch. Identify separate rooms based on function and theme: for example, an herb garden in one part, a terrace in another, a children's play area in a third. Determine how you will enclose or separate each area, making sure you will have adequate screening to provide surprises and discoveries as you move through the garden. Make openings that both frame and invite, and, where appropriate, connect the rooms with paths.

With the structure in place, create style and mood by furnishing rooms with plant material, furniture, and ornament. As you layer on detail, pay attention to the design principles that apply indoors—form, scale, texture, and color—when you choose plants, hardscape material, and ornament and furniture.

The brick squares of a path beneath a laburnum-draped arbor draw eyes and feet to the focal point at the end.

In short, get the "bones" right first. When you do, planting and furnishing will fall into place. You don't need to do the whole scheme at one time. If you're like most gardeners (this one included), you'll take it one room at a time; you may want to perfect just one part of the whole garden. As you embark on a plan, though, it's critical to put in place early such important structural elements as a walk or hedge before you get too detailed in your other planting.

In decorating an interior, I often build a room slowly rather than furnishing it all at once. But if the bones of the room are right—the fireplace and windows are where they should be—adding decoration over time is easy. If the fireplace and windows are in the wrong place, however, I will forever struggle with those obstacles.

Outdoor room concepts may change over time (the rose garden that you would have died for last year suddenly seems far less appealing than a vegetable plot, for instance) but if the basic structure has been sketched out, such changes of heart usually can be accommodated, and costly mistakes, like putting a wall in the wrong place, can be avoided.

PAPER VS. FLOUR

When graph paper leaves you gridlocked, there are a number of different alternatives for sketching out your plan. I have found it useful to simply use stakes and string to demarcate different areas. By adjusting them I eventually achieve the scale and proportion I'm after. Or you can take a sack of flour outdoors and pour a thin line of the stuff where you plan to install a sidewalk or border.

A third possibility is to enlist a willing friend to move a hose around while you view it from a high point such as an attic window. Adjust the hose until you achieve the shape and proportion you're after.

If you're ambitious, you can even mock up a three-dimensional garden with pipe cleaners and cardboard. This approach allows you to envision the elevations of each part of your garden. The great drawback of traditional landscape plans is that they usually include circles of varying sizes that represent mature-sized trees. Circles on the ground don't help all that much when attempting to visualize different views of the garden.

It makes sense to draw elevations of different garden rooms and views so that you can "try on" various schemes. Another great way to do this is to enlarge a photograph (taken straight-on at ground level) of a view you're working on—say, the back of your house. Use tissue paper to lay over it and sketch different possibilities—a pergola attached to the wall, perhaps, or a grouping of redbud trees near the corner of it. I find elevation drawings indispensable in planning interior spaces. Particularly when a client has trouble understanding floor plans, I provide elevation drawings of every room view.

ROOM PLANNING

As you plot out your rooms, keep in mind these few points:

Relate Garden to Architecture
The side or back of your house can become one wall or elevation of a garden room. Since your garden begins at

*This small urban garden in Georgetown, Washington, D.C.,
is a wonderful extension of the wisteria-covered porch.
The relationship of house and garden is perfect, and as you walk
along the paths you come upon beautiful plants, a small pond,
and unusual stone ornaments.*

FORM *The shape of a thing. Form is important in every part of the garden. The shape of a tree determines its usefulness as canopy, or enclosure, or ornament. The form of a stone can contribute to the mood of the garden.*

SCALE *Proportion. Frank Lloyd Wright called a sense of proportion the "diploma Nature gave to the architect."[1] A sensitivity to scale, to the proportionate size of one object relative to another, is one of the most important qualities a gardener uses in building and furnishing garden rooms. Large-scale redwood furniture may overwhelm a small terrace; a tiny ornament may be visually lost in the flowers. Scale matters.*

TEXTURE *The tactile and visual qualities of an object's surface. By "texture" I mean not only the tactile feel of a leaf, but the woven, tapestrylike visual feel of a perennial border.*

MASS *A considerable assemblage or quantity; an expanse of color or tone that defines form or shape in general outline rather than in detail.*

that point, why not drape that wall with climbing hydrangea or Boston ivy?

Also, when you connect a garden to some piece of architecture by proximity, the garden takes on greater strength and character. The first year I bought my house, I found the sunniest spot and tilled it for a vegetable garden. It was near the barn, but it wasn't connected to it. The minute I realized I could connect a greenhouse to the barn and the vegetable plot to the greenhouse, proportioning them appropriately, the whole garden became infinitely more appealing. It seemed to belong there.

Another way in which a garden's design connects and relates to nearby architecture is through the use of an axis. Many formal gardens are organized around a central axis, or line of sight, that emanates from a prominent doorway or window. When you stand in the doorway and look straight ahead, your eye is drawn along a straight visual line to a point in the distance. That line of sight does not have to be reinforced with a straight path, though that is a traditional approach often taken in formal European gardens.

In a French chateau, for example, you may find a doorway centered on the back of the house. From that doorway, one typically walks out onto a terrace, from which you can view a lower garden. The garden is frequently organized symmetrically around a middle pathway that is an axial extension of the central doorway of the home. As you stand at the doorway or on the terrace, your eye is drawn along by the path to some point at which it is stopped—perhaps by a fountain or statue, or by an opening in a distant hedge that leads to a grander view. How much nicer it is to have

your eye immediately drawn to something beautiful rather than nondescript the moment you look out a window or open your back door.

Indoors, hallways are sometimes the organizing axes around which houses are planned. Hallways serve as efficient traffic thoroughfares, with individual rooms placed along them. You can organize your garden in this fashion, too, with a central pathway and garden rooms emanating from it. And just as doorways at either end of the hall are lined up precisely so one has a long view, you can line up doorways outside, too. When building a fence, you might center a gate in relation to your back door, a gate that repeats the shape or some design element of the house's door.

In garden room making, the fun and challenge is to create inviting openings that may reveal something appealing in the distance. This is what I do indoors as well, by placing an interesting painting or desk as a distant focal point that is framed by a doorway.

Build In Visual Delights

In creating rooms, you want to build in surprises. You can achieve this by alternating high and low plantings that block the eye, then open up the view. This principle applies not only to the walls of garden rooms, but in informal settings such as woodland gardens. If you have a meandering path, you'll want to obscure the view when you're making a turn by planting something high at the bend of the path. The view may then open up with lower plantings. For example, you might have a high stand of

Expert garden designer Ryan Gainey renders wonderful drawings of proposed gardens for his clients. A way of doing this yourself is to photograph the landscape, make color copies, and draw in your ideas for adding vertical elements, such as walls, trees, structures or ornaments.

pines in the woods, or have some medium-height rhododendrons through which you walk before coming out to a low clearing of another woodland planting. In open, more informal garden spaces, you need to add tall structure if you lack it, to keep the eye from seeing the whole garden at one time.

Garden making is an exercise in controlling the eye. Building garden rooms involves obscuring ugly views from sight with enclosures, directing the eye through the garden with line and form, attracting the eye with seductive openings, blocking the eye with high interior "walls" that hide the view of the next room, surprising the eye by framing unexpected views, pleasing the eye with rhythmic repetition, and focusing the eye with ornament. Ultimately, the goal of garden room making is a continual visual feast.

Don't Fill In All the Blanks

Be sure to leave void spaces between rooms where possible to provide relief from the texture and busyness of the plantings. It's important to be able to stand back and see what you're doing and what you have. Inside a garden room, you can have an open space in the middle or on the perimeter walkways. And void spaces of grass or ground cover between rooms give you a place to rest your eye before moving to another garden. It's like having a neutral hallway outside of a cluttered living room: It offers visual relief.

Don't Skimp on Proportion

As you lay out your garden, I can't emphasize strongly enough the importance of scale. It's essential not to make the parameters of your garden rooms diminutive in comparison to your house. Especially when a garden is viewed from a distance, the operative philosophy needs to be *bold* rather than delicate.

When I set out to create the formal perennial garden near my house, I knew it was not the time to be timid. The width and length of the beds had to hold up to the scale of a rambling house and the majestic trees around it or they would become invisible. The borders had to occupy a relatively significant piece of ground, they had to be visible from the screened porch, and the whole composition had to balance with the mass of the house. And so, after much tinkering, it does.

ON BUDGETS, CUTTINGS, AND OPTIMISM

If the prospect of pulling together garden rooms seems dauntingly expensive, don't become discouraged. Some of the best gardens I've had the pleasure of seeing have been made over time on a shoestring. Makers of such gardens save money by buying small plant specimens, among other things. The approach requires some patience as tiny shrubs slowly mature into great hedges. But for the patient gardener, pleasure can be found in watching rhythm and form appear, even in a row of very young trees.

Last year I visited the garden of a lovely English lady who had just planted a new area in her knot garden (a series of boxwood parterres laid out in fanciful interwoven patterns). She had taken tiny cuttings of boxwood and made a new section and I was struck by the beauty of it all: her optimism and the charming pattern the little sprigs made.

The connection of elements from house to terrace to vegetable garden works perfectly at this Austin, Texas, residence. The tall cistern covered in lattice and vines is a strong visual feature on the gravel terrace adjacent to the vegetable garden.

The gardens that surround famed textile designer Jack Lenor Larsen's contemporary house on Long Island, New York, are an extension of the architectural style of his home. The elegant pool is set within a hedged garden that can be viewed directly from a window in the house.

Moving directly out from the loggia of the house, this Palm Beach garden is crossed by stone walkways that create areas for delightful pots filled with a variety of plants and standards. The fountain in the center gives a strong visual accent and provides its own lovely music. The garden was designed by George Sanchez.

All gardens need time, and part of the great pleasure of gardening, it seems to me, is watching them mature. I've waited five years for my *Hydrangea petiolaris* to decide whether or not to climb. This year it has, with reckless abandon. And because I had to wait for it, the reward has been especially sweet.

IMAGINE

In the following chapters you'll find ideas for making garden walls, floors, roofs, and passageways, as well as suggestions for decorating garden rooms. But before you get out stakes and string, take a moment to return to those dreams that brought you to gardening in the first place.

Great gardens are full of emotion, planted with the seeds of memory. A waft of magnolia may bring back a childhood in Georgia; the pungent snap of rosemary underfoot can conjure up a honeymoon in Provence. Those emotional cues will be what keep you going as you make your garden.

Think for a moment about how your Eden grows. Does it have a cherry tree shading a wooden bench? Is it fragrant with mock orange blossoms? Does it sprout six kinds of lettuce? Is it silver, blue, white? Entirely green? Must it have a grape arbor or a white picket fence? Is it pots and pots full of topiary shapes? Can it exist without peonies?

What *must* you have in a garden? Go ahead. Imagine.

These perennial borders needed to be wide and long to fit the scale of my garden. The lattice backdrop contains the beds within the landscape; the stone front edging raises them off the ground and provides a strong structural element.

But though an old man, I am but a young gardener.

Thomas Jefferson, in letter to Charles Willson Peale, 1811[2]

II

GOOD BONES MAKE GOOD ROOMS

CHAPTER FIVE: GARDEN WALLS

When Cole Porter penned "Don't Fence Me In" in 1944, he not only summed up the credo of America's cowboys, he also captured the sentiments of many an American gardener. It's not that we lack the native materials to build wonderful garden walls, or that we don't enjoy the enchantment such private oases afford. But as a nation, we are lovers of wide-open spaces. We're enamored of the mountains, the hills, and the plains, and to block the view is nothing short of irreverent. Because we are neighborly people, too, the idea of erecting a fence, particularly a high fence or a wall, strikes some as a bit rude.

Romantic notions aside, though, the reality for many of us is that there's not a great view to be had from where we sit in the backyard. We tend to live in housing clusters, and our vistas are more likely to take in a neighbor's bathroom window than "a ridge where the West commences," as Porter wrote. In such close proximity, it's not unusual to discover that you, too, are part of someone else's view.

If you live close to neighbors and want the privacy and solitude of an outdoor room, you'll need to put up an enclosure. It doesn't have to be an eight-foot-high serpentine brick wall. It may be a green hedge or a low fence with groups of trees and shrubs. You can calibrate your degree of privacy by how high or thick you choose to plant or build your enclosure. But the bottom line is this: It takes walls to make a room.

CLOSING IN THE PLEASURE

Enclosed gardens have been around since the earliest times, springing up in isolated spots and hopscotching across

Boston ivy Parthenocissus tricuspidala *envelops a nineteenth-century iron fence.*

cultures and continents, appearing again and again in gardening history. Wealthy Egyptians surrounded their country villas with huge walls to ward off animals and marauders alike. According to Julia S. Berrall's history *The Garden,* when Persian invaders discovered Egypt's walled gardens in the sixth century B.C., they adapted the idea to their own park tradition, enclosing their groves of trees for seclusion. Centuries later, European knights returned home from the Crusades with new ideas for the walled garden borrowed from the Middle Eastern courts they had observed in their travels.[1] Enclosed gardens were the norm in the Middle Ages. European monks walled their vegetable and herb plots from the outside world. And when the threat of barbaric invasion had passed, medieval families transformed their fortified gardens into outdoor living rooms where they gardened, ate, danced, and bathed in pools.

The walled garden has a glorious past, but what does it have to do with our present lives? Unless you are fortunate enough to have inherited a brick or stone wall, the likelihood of building a high masonry wall is slim. Few gardeners have the means to entirely enclose their outdoor spaces with traditional walls. Our challenge today, instead, is to achieve in affordable ways the intimacy of those historic gardens in our own landscapes.

I think the lesson American gardeners can take from the long tradition of the walled garden is the *value* rather than the method of enclosure. Once the barbarian invaders had departed, interestingly enough, European gardeners continued to enclose their gardens. Why? For the same

Inspiration for a small enclosed garden may be found in this fifteenth-century French engraving, which shows three different fence types: white alba and red gallica roses on a trellis; turf benches with a tunnel arbor covered in vines; and red and white pinks, carnations, and marjoram in the foreground on a lattice fence.

Moisture and color and odor thicken here. The hours of daylight gather atmosphere.

Robert Frost, from "Atmosphere—Inscription for a Garden Wall"[2]

64

Artist unknown, Emilia in Her Garden, *from The Hours of the Duke of Burgndy, 1454-55. Österreichische Nationalbibliothek, Vienna.*

reasons we want enclosures today: to mark the perimeter of the garden, to block out an unsightly view, to frame a *lovely* view, to support a terraced slope, to subdivide a garden into interior rooms, to make a cool oasis in the heat, and especially to provide a measure of privacy in an intrusive world.

How can we American gardeners reconcile our appreciation for wide-open spaces with the idea of enclosure? I believe it's possible to enjoy both. If you want privacy in your outdoor living area yet want to view the landscape beyond it, make your walls semitransparent with strategically placed trees or screens that permit the best of both worlds.

And if you have the luxury of a *glorious* view? Revel in it, cherish it, and don't put your garden in its way. The loveliest prizewinning roses can't compete with a panoramic vista of crashing waves or snowcapped mountains. When I'm in a garden, I want to be immersed in it, undistracted. Likewise when I'm enjoying a magnificent view. Separate the two experiences by placing your garden on the opposite side of your view, or to the side of your home. Then enclose your garden and frame your view with a window in a green hedge or an opening in a fence or wall. The picture will be all the more enchanting for the frame around it.

CHOOSING YOUR BACKDROP
Wall, fence, hedge—which way should you go? Keep in mind the same issues you've faced in every part of the garden plan: What's appropriate with my house and its setting? What can I afford? What do I want an enclosure to do? Imagine the enclosure as it will appear in coming years. Will it be an imposing element in your landscape five years from now, or will it have weathered and disappeared under a cover of clematis and honeysuckle?

Whatever you choose to surround your garden, it will become a backdrop for what's in front of it and will offer a vertical dimension on which to garden.

WALLING THE OUTDOOR ROOM
If you decide on a hard surface rather than trees or shrubs, think of the outside enclosure as an extension of your house's walls. Because you will be adding a permanent structure, the scale and style of the enclosure should relate comfortably to the scale and architectural style of your house. I have a wood house with a stone foundation, for example, so wooden fences and stone walls make sense with it. The simple white picket fence adjacent to the house is intended to be consistent with my home's Federal style. It's useful to pick up detail from the house—an interesting pattern in the porch balustrade, perhaps—and echo it in a fence.

But what do you do if your house lacks detail? Trying to improve the situation with a strongly stylized fence can be risky. An ornate, filigreed Victorian iron fence outside a ranch house will likely point out the comparative plainness of the building rather than enhance its appearance. Instead, observe the building materials and the style of the house. Consider a simpler design with perhaps some very pared down but classic detail.

Contemporary houses, by the way, can look beautiful with a high severe wall of stone or stucco. These can be

Previous page: Blocks of cut stone make a sculptured wall in Roberto Burle Marx's own Rio de Janeiro garden.

CURVED BRICK WALL

neutral or painted a strong color, especially in a climate that has strong sunlight throughout the day. Look at photos of Mexican architect Luis Barragan's brilliant orange and pink stucco garden walls for inspiration.

These are general guidelines I offer. Occasionally creative gardeners ignore a house's architectural features with smashing results. (See "Michael's Garden" at the end of this chapter.)

For the house that does have interesting detail, I see the raising of a fence or wall as an opportunity to gracefully integrate the outdoor room with the rest of the home. The repetition of a ball finial atop a wood post, the reflection of a porch trim pattern in the lattice fence—these are the subtle elements that gather atmosphere in a garden.

MASONRY ENCLOSURES
Partial Masonry Walls
One way to achieve the sense of solidity and permanence a high masonry wall imparts is to top a low stone or brick wall with less expensive materials such as wood or metal. Or build masonry piers and stretch wood or metal or hedge between them. The piers will formalize an entrance, pull the house's architecture out into the garden, and serve as wonderful supports for containers.

If you do a low brick wall, you'll want to match the color of brick and the appearance of the mortar as closely as possible to the house's brickwork, as well as imitate the bond pattern (the way the bricks have been laid), and the general style of your home. Brick looks great near other brick, and that's why it's so at home in city gardens in particular.

Pay attention to mortar, too, as it can be the most noticeable element in a wall's design. Mortar can be used so subtly that a stone wall appears to be dry construction. Or it can ooze from the joints of stones, or mark crazy-quilt boundaries when its color contrasts sharply with the stone's color.

If you want to accentuate the mortar, it should be in a light or contrasting color to the brick or stone. If you want the mortar to recede, it should be close to the color of the material being used or in gray tones.

Because a wall can take on different looks depending on mortar and stone or brick patterns, it's helpful to have a photo or clear mental image from which you're working.

Dry Retaining Walls
When a truck arrived at my home some years ago and dumped two mountains of fieldstone on the lawn, I confess I had some reservations about what I had just done. I wanted a dry stone retaining wall—the kind one sees all over New England—to divide my lawn from a sunken garden I was dreaming about. In the eighteenth and nineteenth centuries, farmers who broke the sod in Connecticut and other eastern states plowed up fieldstones, then formed them into walls along their property lines. Fieldstones were a nuisance to those early farmers, but today a fieldstone wall is regarded as an heirloom by the homeowner who inherits one.

New stone walls are costly to build, but my dear friend Christopher Hewat, an artist and stone wall aficionado, found a farmer who didn't want his wall and was willing to part with it for a sum satisfactory to both of us. I stared at

FIELDSTONE WALL

CUT STONE WALL

69

the stones and tried to discern their flat sides, the part that would face out and form a flat surface. I saw none. Fortunately, Christopher had the vision I lacked to see a wall in the piles of rubble.

Christopher has had a love affair with stone walls since his Connecticut boyhood and has studied many a mortarless, dry stone wall. While he has observed plenty of crudely made walls, occasionally he has come upon a wall that clearly was built by an artist.

Christopher is just such an artist himself. He plays with the stones, arranging and rearranging them, until they have a movement and pattern. Out of those two piles of stones on my lawn, he fashioned a wall that transcends the workmanlike efforts one expects of a stonemason. When he was finished, Christopher left a piece of art in my garden.

What I like about dry stone walls rather than mortared walls is that when you use soil instead of chinking pieces— slivers of stone used to fill in space between the larger rocks—you create yet another surface on which to garden. I've seen daisies cascading from such crevices.

There's nothing delicate about a stone wall; in fact, a tall one can be downright oppressive unless you have lots of space around it. But a low stone retaining wall is friendly, especially when it's topped with a flat stone finishing cap, or coping, which makes an excellent resting place for terra-cotta pots, and gardeners, too. Softened by velvety moss, small succulents, or trailing vines spilling over it, a stone wall can be one of the most picturesque elements in a garden.

If I am enthusiastic about New England dry stone walls, it's because they have become a part of me. But every section of the country has local stone that can be fashioned into walls and paths and piers that are just as attractive. Above all, I think it's important to use the native materials at hand. Every part of the country has master craftsmen, as well, who are romancers of stone. It is worth the effort to seek them out. You will not only get a lovely structure out of it, you will help sustain age-old crafts—whether it's wall building or willow bending or pot making—that very much belong in our gardens today.

Besides fieldstone, quarried rock such as limestone and sandstone is ideal for low garden walls. For example, Fond du Lac cut "dry wall," quarried in Wisconsin and sold by the ton near its source, is a relatively inexpensive but attractive gray-colored limestone that's perfect for dry stone retaining walls. This is one of many comparable kinds of stone available throughout the United States.

A dry stone retaining wall is relatively easy to construct and draws its strength from the weight and friction of one stone upon another. Without mortar, the wall can move freely up and down as the ground freezes and thaws. Because a retaining wall marks a change in elevation and holds back soil, it must be stepped back into that soil during construction.

Even if you're having a stone wall built for you, it pays to visit the stone distributor to choose what you want. There are many variations from which to pick. Some stone has weathered edges and appears more rustic, while others are flat-faced and potentially more formal. Colors, too, will vary depending on the mineral content of the stone. When

My own walled garden gave a sloping lawn its strong design
scheme by creating two levels with wide stairs connecting them.

the stonework is near your house, it makes sense to use stone that approximates your house's color or the stone elements in it.

Stucco

Stucco is one of the most wonderful wall materials and also one of the most underused. It appears in house styles as diverse as Spanish Colonial Revival, Prairie, and New England Colonial. Yet the number of stucco garden walls seems minuscule compared to the prevalence of the material in house construction.

Stucco appeals to me because it accommodates vines so well. And low stucco walls fall into the doable category for the patient and skillful gardener who's willing to research the subject. After you've erected the structure, whether cement block or wood framework, hire an experienced plasterer to apply the stucco, though. It will finish beautifully your structural work. Flat stones or even wood can be used across the top as a coping.

WOOD ENCLOSURES

The Picket Fence

The picket fence, second only to apple pie as an American institution, is actually a descendant of the English paling fence, a simple structure of open vertical boards impaled upon horizontal railings that was introduced by early New England settlers. While they used paling fences to keep wandering cows and horses at bay, today we use them mostly to mark boundaries and distinguish one functional area from another. Americans didn't invent the picket

Simple stucco walls painted in bold color look wonderful in the Southwest and in parts of California and Florida where Mediterranean-style gardens thrive. This Phoenix garden was designed by Steve Martino.

fence, but I think it's fair to say we've made it an art form. Some charming examples of early designs can be seen in Williamsburg, Virginia, where, after 1705, fences were required by law to protect gardens from marauding livestock. Colonial Williamsburg settlers responded to the law with creative gusto, erecting paling, post-and-rail, and wattle fences around their gardens.[3]

Finding an appropriate design for your own garden can be great fun. Naturally, the first place to look is around you at other homes, especially historically significant ones if you have an old house. Some communities have exacting guidelines for picket fences (or any fencing), so it's useful to know what local regulations are before you embark on building one.

For gardeners whose homes go well with Colonial-style designs, you will find a wonderful resource in Peter Joel Harrison's book *Fences*. Peter has spent the past fifteen years searching out and documenting with drawings remaining examples of Colonial-period picket fences, brick designs, gazebos, and other landscaping elements. The result of his labor of love is a series of eighteenth-century-style architectural pattern books, including *Fences,* which contains historic fence and gate designs. Another useful resource is back issues of the *Old-House Journal,* particularly for Victorian designs. Or you can invent your own design. One of the cleverest picket-style fences I've seen featured wood slats that had been cut in the shape of vines. Woven around the wavy pickets were the vines the fence imitated. And for the contemporary house? Build wood fences with very simple lines and no embellishment.

Fence Color

How many times have you stood in a paint store staring at color chips and wondering whether the color you like will make the living room sing—or possibly scream? Choosing a fence color offers the same dilemma (with the added prospect of ribbing from your neighbors for a bad choice). Even if you're contemplating traditional white, think about the square footage the stain will cover before you lift a brush. Is the fence transparent, with spaced pickets, or one long solid surface?

When you choose white, your fence is the brightest thing in your landscape. There are beautiful examples of such fences, but you should anticipate the impact on your garden of a colored fence. In other words, your garden may be about your fence, rather than about what's planted in it. White fences also must be washed or restained from time to time, since they show dirt and wear quickly.

Fortunately, long-lasting stains have made fence painting outmoded. I love the subtle grays, sage greens, and blue-greens available now. And I think deep green on lattice can be a very attractive backdrop. But please note, the key here is *subtlety*. If you like blue, choose gray-blue. And be sure the color relates well with the color scheme of your house.

In general, I think fences are best kept neutral. A high fence that's weathered or stained light gray tends to disappear, and that's ideal if you want a fence for privacy or to block out something. I prefer plants as the dominant feature of the garden, rather than the enclosure.

There are exceptions, of course. In a more contemporary or artistic garden, a fence can be painted a primary or

Pale, n., a narrow board pointed or sharpened at one end, used in fencing or inclosing. This is with us more generally called a picket.

From Noah Webster's Dictionary, 1828

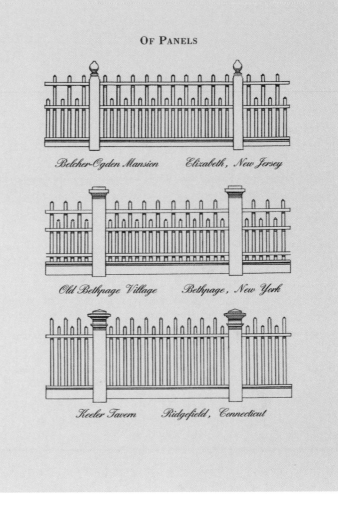

OF PANELS

Belcher-Ogden Mansion Elizabeth, New Jersey

Old Bethpage Village Bethpage, New York

Keeler Tavern Ridgefield, Connecticut

Opposite: Old paling fence from Maine is combined with new posts to surround John Rosselli's vegetable garden in Falls Village, Connecticut. The weathered patina makes it seem as if the garden has always been there.

Above: A selection of historical picket fence designs from Peter Joel Harrison's book Fences: The Architects and Builders Companion for Most Elegant and Useful Designs of Fences, *which is an invaluable source if you are planning to construct a fence.*

strong color to complement an equally strong flower or foliage color. The fence then becomes an ornamental feature or artistic statement.

Finials

Finials are wonderful for dressing up a fence. But beware of choosing too ornate a design for a simple scheme. Sometimes all you need is a cap on top of each post to give the fence an elegantly finished look.

Flea markets are great sources for old wood finials. I have collected them over the years and have had several designs reproduced by a woodturner for my own fences. On the lattice screens backing the formal garden's borders, tall and classically shaped urns fit the bill, while in the kitchen garden I've used fat, squat finials that remind me of Mughal urns.

Wood Privacy Fences

Early twentieth-century garden writers regularly bemoaned the prevalence of "old style" wood fences, the high solid closed-board fences their grandparents used along backyard property lines. They were referring to the "privacy" fences we erect today, the six- to eight-foot stockade and board fences that we buy in sections from our garden centers.

While some minor improvements have been made to stock wood fences, they still can look oppressively dismal. But the fact is, they do the job, as they did for our great-grandparents, when budget is a constraint and privacy is a necessity. By placing large square posts between the panels and adding a cap or finial to the post, you can dress up the basic board fence to look quite civilized. Decorate it further either by placing wire grids on top of the fence to support vines or covering the fence with lattice for the same purpose.

You can also color it. Stain the closed-board fence a medium gray. Then place over it a lighter gray-stained lattice. You can also create this effect using only one stain color. I recently saw a fawn beige closed-board privacy fence with a subtly scalloped top. Over each fence section was placed a series of rectangular lattice panels with arched tops, stained the same color and mirroring the gentle curves of the fence.

You might want to color your privacy fence with living green. Place columnar evergreens, such as arborvitae, in front of the intermittent support posts, and in between those paint the stockade fence with climbing hydrangea or Virginia creeper or espaliered fruit trees. The fence itself can weather or be stained dark green.

Fruit trees have traditionally been espaliered against sunny walls in order to quickly ripen the fruit. Many different training patterns exist for espaliered trees and these patterns are decorative as well as functional. If you don't want to prune and shape a tree from scratch, you can purchase espaliered fruit trees that have already been started at a nursery.

Lattice

It's no wonder lattice fencing has long been a staple in gardens around the world. Ever since some ancient gardener figured out that upright frames with crossed

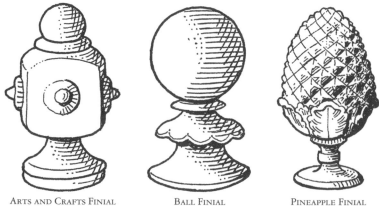

ARTS AND CRAFTS FINIAL   BALL FINIAL   PINEAPPLE FINIAL

Far left: One of my favorite finials on my kitchen garden fence was copied from an antique one I found that reminded me of Mughal Indian architecture.

Left: On the lattice in my perennial border, I used this elongated Federal-style finial, which comes from the same period as my house.

Above: An easy solution for privacy is the stockade fence. Letting it weather to a natural color makes it seem a part of the land, and the simple gate makes the wall less intimidating; the fence is also a nice backdrop for planting.

Layered enclosures are made with a beautifully designed post-and-rail fence by artist and gardener extraordinaire Robert Dash. The oval window placed in the lattice screen creates a special frame for your eye.

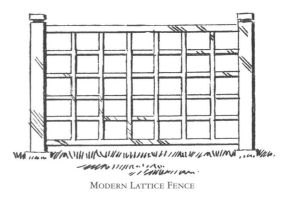

MODERN LATTICE FENCE

wood pieces served handily to support vine tendrils, gardeners in Asia, Europe, and the Americas have embellished upon the concept.

Lattice is practical yet elegant. It's light yet gives a sense of solidity when it's well built. And because of its airy feel, one can make a high enclosure of it without the expense of a masonry wall or the potentially oppressive feeling of a closed-board privacy fence.

Lattice fence construction was once an art in which skilled carpenters used furniture-quality joinery to make architectural lattice. This type is still being made by a few companies (see Resources), though it's more expensive than most commercially available lattice options. Wood pieces are notched together to produce a flat, not overlaid, surface.[4]

Today there seems to be a hierarchy in the world of lattice fencing. At the high end is the beautifully constructed, furniture-quality trelliswork just mentioned. Less expensive but of high quality is custom-made cedar lattice, which is overlaid, then epoxied or stapled at the connecting points. Some custom makers of lattice use heavy three-quarter-inch-thick cedar strips to create lattice that is one and a half inches thick at the point where the wood strips are overlaid. Finally, there's the prefabricated lattice panel one finds at building supply centers, where thicknesses can run to a thin half inch or less. I prefer a thicker lattice. There's nothing more slapdash-looking than a flimsy fence of lattice set precariously into the earth.

If you're handy, a lattice fence is a very possible do-it-yourself endeavor. But go for the heaviest weight you can afford, and make certain your pressure-treated posts are sunk down to the frost line in cold climates. Then finish the posts with a cap or a cap plus ball finial. You can stain the fence in a color related to your house or let it weather to a gray.

A diagonally crossed lattice pattern tends to adapt itself to traditional settings, while a grid pattern can look terrific near a modern house. And a lattice fence seems to cry out for decorative gates and arbors set into it, making it one of the more fun garden projects to contemplate.

If you don't want an entire fence of it, consider the clever lattice screen. Employing the same sturdy construction techniques used for fences, you can set a pair of lattice screens opposite each other on a long lot to provide privacy in specific open spots. Or space two or three screens along the sunny side of a garden to make a rose-covered barrier. Or make a hiding place for garbage cans and other necessities by placing a screen in front of an existing fence.

I've used long, free-standing sections of lattice as backdrops behind the two symmetrical perennial borders that face one another in my formal garden. They're set a few feet in front of the lilac hedges on either side of the garden, creating hallways behind them, and walls for two sides of the garden.

Into the Woods

There are other choices in wood fencing besides the more predictable picket, lattice, or stockade fence. If you have a rustic house in the country, whether Montana or Virginia, simple fences of cut timber, with the bark still on, make wonderful enclosures. These post-and-rail fences can be

TRADITIONAL LATTICE FENCE

constructed in a zigzag fashion as well as straight. By splicing and mitering the same cut timbers, you can create chinoiserie lattice patterns in a fence, thus formalizing a basically rustic fence material.

Though I have a formal house and the fences are made in a formal style, I chose a natural gray post-and-rail fence to surround the perimeter of my property. The rustic fence has an informal feeling that is consistent with the countryside.

Wattle is rustic fencing with a different mood—very English. Woven of willow branches, it has a basketlike appearance and looks wonderful in a country garden or as a backdrop for a kitchen garden. English wattle (also known as hurdle) fencing is now available in the United States in six-foot-wide panels that are two, four, and six feet high. (See Resources.) In the tiny garden at Treillage, we topped a low stone wall with a screen of wattle fencing, raising the height of the wall and blocking an unsightly view. It created a beautiful rustic texture for that spot.

Yet another rustic possibility is a simple stick fence. Fashioned of thin saplings as palings and cut irregularly to emphasize its simplicity, a stick fence is pure charm around a vegetable garden.

Entirely different in its light, Japanese feel is the bamboo garden screen. It works with contemporary houses as well as Japanese garden schemes because of its clean lines. Especially nice is woven bamboo. If you live in an area where bamboo is natural— in the South or near a California beach—there's nothing prettier than a bamboo fence as it ages to a gray.

METAL FENCES
Iron Fences
While iron fences are manufactured today, I think there's great charm to be had by integrating pieces of old iron fencing into your garden's enclosure. Sections of iron fencing can be alternated with hedges, or placed between masonry pillars, or hung against a garage wall as trellis. Ornamental iron work adds elegance and character when it's used well.

Wrought-iron fences were once a symbol of prosperity in nineteenth-century America. When numerous foundries in the United States began offering cast-iron fencing at more affordable prices, middle-class Victorians (there were catalog shoppers in those days, too) soon took to enclosing their properties with the fancy new models. By the turn of the century, though, the passion for iron fences had diminished, and during World War I many a fence was turned into scrap metal for the war effort. There is still available a supply of these antiques through architectural salvage companies, usually costing between fifteen and twenty-five dollars per running foot. The examples we see today are often a combination of both wrought-iron and cast-iron with, for example, wrought-iron pickets and cast-iron finials. The finials might be shaped as crosses or fleurs-de-lis.

It's not impossible to locate a complete, intact antique iron fence—it just takes some persistence. But *sections* of iron fences are easier to find. Most wrought- or cast-iron fences will have been painted, to protect against rust. If you purchase iron fencing that's rusty, it will need to be cleaned

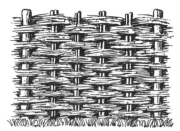

WATTLE FENCE

A rustic twig fence in chinoiserie style surrounds a New England rose garden. The romantic quality is enhanced by the simple evergreen background that also serves as a screen. The fence and garden were designed by Nancy McCabe for Elise Lufkin.

ELABORATE VICTORIAN IRON FENCE

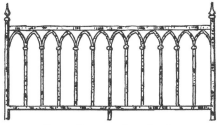

SIMPLE VICTORIAN IRON FENCE

of all foreign substances, then painted with a rust-resistant primer and an oil-based final coat. Since paint on old ironwork often contains lead and presents an environmental hazard, it's best to have it stripped professionally rather than to sandblast it yourself.

There is a range of iron fence styles, from Gothic to rustic. Try to remain consistent with the feeling of your house when it comes to the ornateness of the fence. While iron fences don't provide privacy, they work well as decorative elements near clean, simple, and uncomplicated plantings or lawn. But put a decorative iron fence around a kitchen garden or perennial garden and you end up with too many busy elements.

If you want a new iron fence or gate, there are old fence companies in the United States still producing their early designs. (See Resources.) And though an iron fence is a bigger investment than a wood model, it is guaranteed to last much longer.

Chain Link (And How to Hide it)
A chain-link fence, unfortunately, looks like a prison enclosure. My best advice to someone who has one is to take it down. It may be an inherited fence, it may even be one of those early landscaping mistakes you made when you still thought humus was a Middle Eastern vegetable dip. If the latter is true, forgive yourself, then yank it out. But if the chain-link barrier belongs to a neighbor who's fond of it, or if your budget rules out fence demolition, don't despair. You can obscure it in a number of ways.

Perhaps the easiest way of concealing a chain-link fence is to cover it with plantings or another, slightly higher fence. If you have a traditional house, for example, you might place a picket fence in front of the entire length of metal fence and wire it in place. Chain link makes a great support for lattice, English hurdle, and bamboo fencing, too. Lengths of stock lattice fencing, stained or weathered gray, will give you quite a transformation for your money.

You can soften the chain-link fence with plant material in a couple of ways. The simplest is to train vines to cover the chain link. 'Heavenly Blue' morning glories, with deep green, heart-shaped leaves, are wonderful.

A more formal disguise can be concocted, though. For every metal post supporting the chain-link fence (usually every six feet or so), plant evergreens. Or you may want to conceal the metal posts by placing in front of each a four-by-four-inch pressure-treated wood post, topped with a ball finial or a simple pyramid-shaped cap. Then cover the chain link in green, either with espaliered euonymus— which grows like a weed—or an evergreen hedge of yew or hemlock. A fast-growing, inexpensive shrub is easy to prune as a wall of green. With wonderful posts stained gray or painted to match the trim color of the house—perhaps dark green or wine red—you will have connected the enclosure back to the house.

LIVING WALLS: HEDGES AND GREEN SCREENS
Because the high-walled garden is unattainable for most of us, it makes sense to create walls with hedges and trees. So much has been written about the wonderful varieties of trees and shrubs available to use as living enclosures that you may

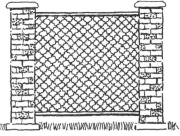
BRICK AND CHAIN-LINK FENCE

Clematis montana rubens *charms an otherwise unappealing chain-link fence.*

be confused about which to choose for your own garden.

How to proceed? Think in shapes first. What form do you want a mature planted wall to take? Do you see a tall, boxlike mass surrounding your garden? Do you see a block of green only above the fence line, with intermittently spaced trunks forming a pattern along an exposed fence? Do you see vase-shaped river birches with white bark, staggered irregularly along the property line and underplanted with daffodils? Do you see a semitransparent wall of scattered trees that allows you to borrow the view beyond while giving you the illusion of enclosure? Or do you envision an arrangement of dwarf conifers in a spectrum of shapes and shades of green from yellow to blue?

If you want a traditional hedge, most often it will consist of the same plant placed in a row. Different trees lend themselves to different purposes. Clipped hemlock or yew will give you a severe line—perfect for privacy or as a backdrop for an herbaceous border because the green extends to the ground. Lilacs, on the other hand, offer a softer, looser, less formal look. They are sentimental favorites with gardeners for their fragrance, shape, and color, but they're not the best candidates for privacy or as a backdrop to a border.

Formal and Informal Approaches
By uniformly planting in a row the same variety of tree—and planting enough of that variety—you can create one green mass *above* the trunks.

The straight line can be formalized further with a technique called pleaching that has been employed in

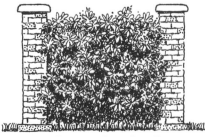

VINES COVERING CHAIN-LINK FENCE

A fence made of espaliered fruit trees against a bright blooming hedge of azalea at the Ladew Topiary Gardens in Monkton, Maryland. This sort of living fence also looks wonderful against a wall or simple board fence.

Espaliered fruit trees around terra-cotta pipe couplings add interest to an otherwise ordinary stucco wall—and have the added bonus of bearing delicious fruit.

Espalier, n., a trellis or framework on which fruit trees and shrubs are trained to grow flat; v., to train on an espalier.

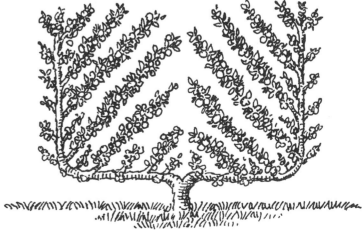

ESPALIERED FRUIT TREE

85

traditional gardens for centuries to create an architectural effect. Pleaching involves the intertwining of lateral branches as the trees grow (sometimes wood or wire frameworks are used to help along this process). Once the branches have grown together, the mass of greenery can be clipped into one continuous form. A high platform on wheels is required for an annual trimming of the trees. Rows of pleached trees have been called "stilted hedges," a term that aptly describes the pencillike tree trunks beneath a thick green block above.

Hornbeam, beech, and lime trees are traditional choices for pleaching in formal settings, but not the only options. I have seen pleached laurel trees used very effectively as privacy barriers between homes in California.

Many settings call for a far more informal approach. I think outer boundary plantings on country properties look far better when they imitate how trees grow in nature, rather than as a straight row of, say, white pines. Also, by staggering trees and shrubs in more informal settings, you can create privacy where you need it, and openings to borrow views where you can.

If you want a formal hedged garden near your country home, you can still have it. But for outer property hedges, go for a more natural look.

Before you embark on planting a living wall, sit down with some books and study the shapes of trees and shrubs. Observe the specimens that flourish in your climate. Talk to someone at your local nursery, agricultural extension service, or nearby botanical garden. Describe the shape and effect you want to achieve and find out which varieties like the kind of weather and soil you have. Educate yourself about what's involved in maintaining a particular look.

INTERIOR WALLS

Fences, hedges, and walls are not only for keeping the world at bay. They can define interior rooms within the larger scheme. Often the natural contours of a landscape will suggest individual rooms. Or the footprint of the house itself, the way it is situated on the land, will suggest possible divisions of the garden.

English gardeners delight in dividing up their gardens with hedges, for good reasons. It's cheaper to put in a live hedge than to build a garden wall, and it's a more natural and attractive solution than a stockade fence, particularly when one sees both sides of the interior wall.

If you are an impatient gardener with an accommodating budget, you can install a six-foot-tall, forty-five-foot-long mature hemlock hedge, balled and burlaped upon arrival, for roughly nine thousand dollars. At the other end of the spectrum, the patient gardener who's willing to wait can make a hedge for substantially less.

WINDOWS IN THE WALL—FRAMING THE VIEW

Have you ever noticed that mullions—those wood dividers between windowpanes—sometimes *enhance* your view of the outdoors? They are reminders that, while you are not in the garden, you are nonetheless experiencing it in a different but pleasurable way. Windows focus the eye, and when there's a view worth looking at, the effect is akin to looking at a framed work of art.

PLEACHED TREES

You can make openings in your outdoor walls quite easily. If your neighbor has a beautiful stand of birches beyond your hedge or fence, by all means borrow the view. Cut a square or round shape into the hedge, or simply leave an opening at the appropriate spot.

I tend to associate these openings with formal settings, such as the hedged garden at Cranbourne in England, where two magnificent perennial borders lie within the four high green walls. In and of itself, the room is breathtaking. But because the meadow beyond is also very beautiful, the gardeners have framed the view with windows in the hedges. And somehow, because you have to peek at it, the view of the meadow is all the more special.

MICHAEL'S GARDEN

What makes a garden magic? In Michael Trapp's, it is the elements of intense privacy, delightful surprise, and a profound sense of place created by the walls of his garden. Enter Michael's garden and you feel you've stumbled onto a ruined villa where generations of gardeners have left remnants of their efforts behind. A seventeenth-century Venetian stone door lintel serves as edging for one of the raised beds; iron Victorian bridge finials mark the corners of the pond; a huge terra-cotta Corinthian capital, scavenged from a demolished Ohio hospital, sits comfortably amid irises. Raised beds fairly bursting with perennials recall an English garden, and yet, you think, this place has a Mediterranean feel. Italian, perhaps. Or is it French? One thing is certain: It doesn't feel like the backyard of a house/antique shop in Cornwall, Connecticut.

Michael Trapp, antique dealer and garden maker extraordinaire, has concocted an Eden on three-quarters of an acre of lopsided terrain, and much of its magic is owed to the structural elements he has woven around and into the garden. Privacy is absolute here, achieved with a variety of walls, many of which are architectural fragments loaded with historical allusion.

Faced with a lot that split itself into an upper and lower level, Michael divided his garden into three rooms: a large brick paved main garden with raised beds adjacent to his home and shop, another smaller hedged room on the same level, and a shaded glen on the lower level.

What holds the garden together is its delicate bones. In the main upper garden, a wall of lattice containing an old pair of arched louvered doors obscures a parking area. In front of the lattice, tall junipers alternate with nineteenth-century wood columns. The lattice, doors, and columns are a washed-out white—faded, it seems, by decades of benign neglect.

At the end of the parallel brick paths that run between the raised beds and rectangular pool, you are stopped by an old curved balustrade. The weathered wood railing overlooks the Housatonic River (or is it the Tiber?) and suggests an Italian belvedere where one stands for a scenic view.

Michael has connected the sunny upper garden to the shaded one below with a slip of a wall, a wood colonnade that leads the visitor down stone steps into a glen. Limestone rocks, scavenged from a nearby mountain, support a terraced hill on one side, while a woven stockade fence subtly blends into the opposite hilltop. The tiny lower garden is entirely

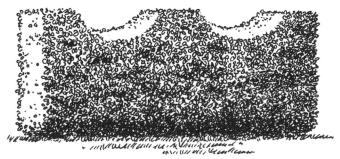

SCALLOPED HEDGE

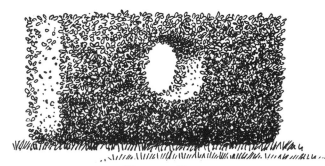

WINDOW IN HEDGE

secluded, with a central path bordered by low stone walls and appointed symmetrically with large olive jars from Crete. One lingers here, amid a profusion of hostas, half expecting the chance appearance of a garden nymph.

Up the far steps you pass through a wonderful curving hallway of arborvitae that leads to an arbor trained over with apple trees. Here you find the third outdoor room, a grassy lawn surrounded by a seven-foot-high euonymus hedge, which serves as a green for summer croquet games.

One might question how balustrades, lattice screens, hedges, and a stockade enclosure relate to a "Victorianized" Greek revival house. Not at all, says Michael, who felt liberated from pursuing architectural consistencies by the architectural inconsistency of the house itself. Nonetheless, a single vision holds the entire scheme together. Steeped in classic references, surrounded by walls that exclude the Colonial flavor of the neighborhood, woven together by interior ribbonlike walls, and connected thematically indoors and out by architectural artifacts and ornaments, Michael's garden is a world unto itself.

What is perhaps most extraordinary about his achievement is the fact that Michael brought the garden to its current state of loveliness on a limited budget, in a short five years. By using local stone and brick, by scouring salvage companies for the rest, and by doing the construction work himself, Michael proved that money does not an Eden make; rather, it's the spirit and sweat of a motivated gardener who's not afraid to imagine.

Native fieldstone walls form the terraces of Michael Trapp's hillside garden. The terracing gives the hill structure and creates many areas for planting, while the large Tuscan oil jars define the entryway and lead your eye deep into the garden.

CHAPTER SIX:
THE GARDEN FLOOR

I wish that my room had a floor
I don't so much care for a door
But this running around
Without touching the ground
Is getting to be such a bore.

Gelett Burgess, "The Floorless Room"[1]

When it comes to living in the garden, even paradise can use a floor plan. Think of the garden floor as you do the blueprint of a house—it outlines how you will live in that space. That's why it's so useful to have the garden floor sketched out before the trees and gravel trucks arrive. It forces you to think through critical issues before you begin. How will foot traffic move through the space? How can openings be lined up to provide a long view? Which rooms will be large or small and how will they be used?

Lines and shapes define the rooms of your garden, as they do in the house's plan. These lines on the floor—the perimeter of the terrace, the straight or serpentine path, the shape of the lawn—not only mark one area from another but also exert their own power on the landscape. The long line of a path or driveway pulls your eye along with it.

Bedding lines, for example, are strong graphic elements on the garden floor. You can pull down an arch or line from the architecture of your house and echo it in the outline of a bed. And repeated lines adjacent to each other impose structure on the ground. A curving mass of liriope, for example, outlined with the same curve in a stone path and adjacent lawn, makes for rhythmic movement.

The material you choose for these shapes are as important as the shapes themselves, especially when there's a large mass of it. The form, texture, and color of the material will affect the feel of your garden and determine whether that feature will stand out or lie soft in the landscape, whether it will be restful to your eye, or pleasingly dramatic, or simply irritating.

A graphic checkerboard terrace made with squares of grass and cast cement pavers. This simple design can complement almost any style of house.

TERRACES

The garden floor begins the moment your feet hit the ground outdoors—and often, the world over, that's on a terrace. Traditionally the terrace has been an elevated platform adjoining the house that permits the viewer to look down on the garden. With roots in Italian villas where the terrace connected the house with a sloping hillside, and in formal French gardens where it was an imposing architectural extension of the home (or palace), today the terrace is more of an outdoor living room where we can sit and admire our efforts. It comes in many permutations: elevated or flat on the ground, squared off or curving, open to the sky or covered by a pergola, enclosed by elegant stone balustrades or charmingly simple, like the dirt terraces covered with fine pea gravel and flower pots one sees in France and Italy.

The terrace works as a large visual element in the landscape, a sort of platform grounding the house to the land. And because it is a transitional spot, part house and part garden, you want the elements of both worlds to blend comfortably. One early English garden designer recommended that terraces should be the size of one of the rooms out of which you have just stepped. This is one way to think about the terrace's size. Its use is another. And certainly the relative size of the house should be taken into consideration when planning the scale of the terrace.

Especially because it is adjacent to the house, the terrace should look as if it belongs there, and for that reason, you'll want to tie in the terrace's building materials and colors with those used in the house.

It's nice to create a mood on the terrace—elegant enough, perhaps, for Mitzi Gaynor and Rozanno Brazzi to waltz across some enchanted evening. Or simply welcoming and comfortable, in the way a favorite room is. Whatever picture you're after, you need to tune your eye to the differences that seemingly small design choices make. On the terrace, it's the paving material that often sets the mood.

Stone Terraces

Native stone is perfect flooring for the terrace, gracefully making the transition from the house into the garden. Stone is eminently adaptable in most situations. It can be civilized—cut into regular geometrical forms—and laid neatly edge-to-edge for a clean, formal appearance. Or it can arrive at your house *au naturel* and settle into the terrace in a charmingly loose fashion.

"Flagstone," a common terrace choice, refers simply to the paving stone indigenous to an area and can be a number of different stones, including limestone, sandstone, and slate.[2] Snapped from the quarry in shallow slabs, it's typically available in sections approximately two inches thick and around two by three feet wide. In the East, bluestone is often used for paving; in the West, buff or rose Colorado sandstone is a favorite. Within one geographical region, there will be several variations on the flagstone theme. Surface textures and colors can run the gamut. In the Midwest, the standard gray-white color one associates with flagstone, for example, will range from yellow to pinkish tones. And exterior edges for different types can be jagged or nearly smooth.

"How a stone looks was determined eons ago by what

This Japanese-inspired raised wooden path makes an intriguing
element on the floor of a contemporary garden.

This marvelous terrace combines bluestone squares with brick laid around the stones. The moss grows quickly in the sand-filled spaces, giving the impression that the terrace has been there for centuries.

The cool white tile terrace on the loggia of this serene house creates an aura of Zen-like calm as you view the pond and trees beyond.

Mother Nature cooked up that day," an architect colleague recently commented while studying a dizzying array of stone choices for a house. The interaction of molten minerals and gases heated up and pressurized inside the earth thousands of years ago has gifted each area of the country with wonderful local color.

In planning terraces, paths, and retaining walls, it makes sense to stick with Mother Nature's regional recipes. The closer you adhere to the color palette of native stone, the more natural your terrace is likely to look. Even in selecting stone for an interior fireplace, I use what's native to a location. Recently I specified Rocky Mountain granite in a Boulder client's fireplace. There's a visual continuity that results when your eyes travel from the fireplace to the landscape outside the windows. One has a sense that the house is a part of its site.

The color of the terrace is particularly important because it adjoins the house. Bluestone, which varies in color from green to cool gray-blue to brownish gray, is often selected for terraces because it has a relatively flat surface that accommodates snow shoveling. Before you buy it, though, bring home several pieces and view it where it will be placed. I prefer warm brown tones in bluestone; it looks more weathered and neutral.

By virtue of its origins, local stone is less expensive than other rock trucked in to your area, but don't assume that fact narrows your choices to one option. Take a field trip to the stone yard to discover the possibilities. In short, when ordering up a flagstone terrace, it's wise to trust your own eye as much as that of the contractor you've hired.

On the bricks the green moss grew,
Yellow lichen on the stone,
Over which red apples shone;
Little war that castle knew.

William Morris, "Golden Wings"[3]

Patterns

In making a terrace, because you're paving a larger area than a path, it's visually pleasing to break up the mass with pattern—the bigger the terrace, the bigger the pattern. If you have French doors centered on the terrace, for instance, you can create a pattern in the middle of it. Or you may want to use a decorative element, such as colorful tiles or a millstone in the center. What you want to avoid is a big slab of concrete that resembles a mall.

With a contemporary house, a simple terrace might be made with large cut stone or poured concrete. The concrete terrace will look more interesting if it has been scored with lines or surrounded by brick or a natural stone border to soften it.

If you have limited terrace space and you're using brick, try a chevron pattern to trick the eye and make it look longer. If you're doing a patterned path of two materials such as brick with a stone border, you'll want to use the same pattern on the terrace, but again, you might enlarge the pattern there according to its scale.

Beautiful paving patterns can also be made with pebbles of different colors set in concrete. Among the oldest and most universally used paving methods, pebble terraces and walks result from artfully placing into mortar stones or shells that are found near at hand. And whether it's a courtyard in China or in Miami Beach, the technique adds an incomparable texture to a setting. I recall seeing streets in Vence, France, inlaid with jewel-like pebble designs of vases, flowers, and other interesting patterns such as basketweave or geometries.

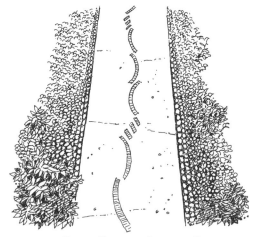

PEBBLE DESIGN IN CONCRETE PATH

Texture

In my own home and garden, in choosing a writing table for a guest bedroom or picking out brick for the front walkway, patina counts. I prefer the nicks and mellow color that age confers. This is one point of view and certainly not the only scenario for other people or other settings. But in my own New England landscape, I like the softness of materials that look weathered and old. Part of an aged look comes from a brick's color or a stone's irregular shape, but plants endow softness, too.

With a very informal terrace of flagstone, for example, you can plant thyme, golden oregano, wild strawberries, even lady's mantle and lavender between the stones. The foliage softly blends and helps make a transition from the terrace to the lawn and greenery around it. Also consider leaving a couple of boxed-in spaces about one foot deep for planting vines between the wall of the house and the beginning of the terrace. Vines don't require much room at ground level, and give back a hundredfold in beauty what they take up in space.

Soft Concrete

Even concrete terraces can be softened by adding color pigment when mixing or by working tint into the top surface. You can also take the hard edge off concrete by texturing it while wet with any number of tools, from trowels to brooms.

Chemical stains, which can be used on old terraces and walks as well as new, are brushed or sprayed on concrete to create a variety of effects, including the aged, mottled look of natural stone. And because the stain reacts chemically with the concrete, the color penetrates a quarter inch into the surface and won't peel off like paint.

There is a caveat to this information on staining, though. Like the TV commercials in which a pitchman performs some wild stunt, then adds, "I am a trained professional. Do not try this at home," the same thing can be said of staining concrete. The stains are indelible, both on pavement and clothing, so use them at your own risk. The most successful applications of concrete staining are often done by experienced professionals.

DECKS

More than any other part of the garden floor plan, the terrace requires a consistency of materials and design to make the blend between house and garden succeed. We need only look at the ubiquitous redwood deck to understand why consistency—at least as it extends to the terrace—is not the hobgoblin of small minds.

The deck is the great American *faux pas.* You see them everywhere, hanging off the backs of traditional houses across the land, looking for all the world like the prows—in fact, the decks—of boats. Lacking any connection with the houses to which they are attached, they are often raised well above ground level and don't connect with the garden, either.

When elevated on flat and open land, all the deck's a stage, and you and your family are the poor players upon it. The audience: your neighbors. If you've ever tried to enjoy a family moment on an elevated deck in an unenclosed yard, you know how it feels—something akin to sharing vacation

This wooden deck is very well conceived with three lattice pergolas to support climbing vines. The space is further softened with pots of flowering plants adorning the steps.

pictures with a stranger. Here's my husband, George, in his bathrobe having coffee. Here I am in my bathing suit. Here are our kids having hot dogs. On such a platform, one is inclined to fret, "How are we doing?"

Wooden decks can look spectacular with contemporary-style houses or floating out over a sand dune. They don't look great floating out over an expanse of grass in Illinois. Decks can look great when they extend a contemporary house out into the treetops in hilly terrain. They don't look great in a suburban development elevated above an open stretch of commonly shared land that's flat as a pancake. Decks look more natural if they lead to some natural area, such as a prairie garden or into the sand, rather than into a stretch of lawn.

Popularized in the fifties with modular contemporary housing that was low to the ground, they are inappropriate with eighteenth- and nineteenth- and many twentieth-century houses. Nonetheless, the deck has become American vernacular for "terrace," regardless of house style. And in most cases, it's a boat out of water.

Addressing the Raised Foundation

Everyone wants a place to sit outside, and a deck is a cheaper option than others. If you have a wood house with an elevated foundation, you may feel a deck is your only solution for gaining an outdoor living area. But by paying attention to construction details and materials, rather than opting for the standard redwood open-board models, you can create a wooden structure that earns the appelation "terrace" rather than "deck."

Imagine a Victorian house with an elevated foundation. Rather than the standard four-by-four posts often used in deck construction, use larger, more massive columns (these can be hollow) that will relate better to the house's scale. You can build these of wood or use stucco, brick, or stone if it's appropriate and you can afford it. Below floor level, stretch lattice between the piers to give that plane a solid surface and to enclose the lower part of the structure. (You can use wood slats or square grid-shaped lattice with a modern house.) Above the floor, stretch a balustrade and railing that allows a view. Make this as transparent and low as building code permits. Add an arbor above the window line, if you choose. Then stain the new terrace to tie in with the color scheme of your house. Plant vines and shrubs and roses against the lattice backdrop. You have created, in essence, an open porch that's sympathetic with your Victorian home, and a whole lot more attractive than the typical redwood deck.

Another option for the house on an elevated foundation is to raise the level of the earth and create a "true" terrace. If you are building a new home and want terraces, it makes sense, while bulldozers are at the site, to contour the earth around the house by shaping terraces there, supported by retaining walls.

STEPS

Who thinks of stairs as a romantic element of the garden? Not many of us. Indoors it's an easier association to make. We have classic film settings to cement that connection: Clark Gable carrying Vivien Leigh up the stairs at Tara in

Stand on the highest pavement of the stair —
Lean on a garden urn —
Weave, weave the sunlight in your hair —.
T. S. Eliot, "La Figlia che Piange"[4]

Gone With the Wind; Audrey Hepburn, swathed in red silk, floating down a white marble staircase in *Funny Face.* It's a romantic association we still embrace. Homebuilders today are often called upon to build in elegant staircases, despite the fact that grand entrances went the way of bone corsets and ball gowns about a century ago.

Outdoors, few of us have terraced villas of the classic Italian sort that lend themselves to staircases. Yet, if your property has even a small change in elevation, you have an opportunity to capture some of the magic presence that grander staircases suggest. And aside from making inclines navigable, steps offer themselves up as ideal spots for sitting and viewing the garden as well as for placing containers and ornaments.

I was inspired to put some character into my own garden's steps after seeing Emilio Pucci's Italian villa in a magazine. It included a whole terrace consisting of vast grass steps, the long horizontal lines of which were edged with stone. The boldness of Pucci's design was breathtaking and encouraged me to try it on a smaller scale.

The grass and limestone steps in my garden lead from a lawn through the retaining wall and down into the formal garden. Flanked on each side by stone lions, the grass treads are shallow and broad, requiring two footfalls at each spot. It's a conscious attempt to slow down one's pace, and to encourage visitors to linger a moment and enjoy the view.

While outdoor steps ordinarily connect to paths, a set of stairs can stand alone as well. The planners of America's early-twentieth-century estate gardens sometimes used steps, unattached to walkways, to punctuate an open space.

Back in 1948, the great American landscape designer Fletcher Steel laid out these beautiful steps in a woodland garden in Massachusetts. The design translates perfectly to our own woodland gardens today.

Next page: If your property is in or near the woods, nothing can be more beautiful than meandering paths over moss-covered ground with sunlight filtering through the trees. The occasional placement of ornaments or containers can also enhance the experience, as it does in the Rockefeller garden in Northeast Harbor, Maine.

This effect can be seen at the formal Filoli Gardens in Woodside, California, where the white of a simple set of three or four steps glows in a vast green lawn.

Keep step material consistent with the nearby walkway's material or the mood of your house if it's close by. Stone and brick make wonderful treads when edged in the same or contrasting materials. And earth-colored decomposed granite works as tread material for concrete risers that have been poured in place.

Wood steps are often used in rustic settings to make a transition down an incline. For some reason, gardeners are hooked on creosoted railroad ties, which I find distinctly unappealing. But like many things, our eyes become so accustomed to them we don't stop to ask ourselves, "Is this the best I can do?" There are alternatives. Split logs of untreated wood stripped of their bark are quite pretty, as are simple cut timber risers that weather to a silver-gray.

It almost goes without saying that moss adds magic to stone steps, softening the look and somehow making them more welcoming. You can enhance the effect by inserting low-growing plants between the stones (low enough not to trip people), and by painting the risers with a wonderful ground cover such as purple-leaved *Ajuga reptans* or creeping *euonymus*, creating a wonderful horizontal striped pattern.

PATHS

Paths are outdoor hallways that move traffic and connect individual rooms. Indoors, you want a hallway to offer the most direct route, but outside in the private garden, taking the long way may be exactly what you have in mind. And just as indoor hallways set the axes for a house, paths work as fundamental structural elements that direct you through the garden and into its individual rooms.

The whole point of a path is to walk on it, and, regardless of its beauty, if it doesn't work, it's useless. For a main walkway the width should accommodate two people walking side by side to comfortably pass along it. A less traveled auxiliary path can be narrower, perhaps just a few stepping-stones.

Practicality will drive your path decisions as much as aesthetics. You want to be able to shovel snow off of a main walkway, and to walk on it without tripping, so the surface can't be too irregular, and good drainage is needed to avoid puddles. A gravel path, for example, is an impractical choice as a main artery in cold climates if you want a shoveled surface, but works well as an auxiliary route in the warm months. (I've laid a brick path to the front door, a gravel path to the kitchen garden, and I mow paths through the grass to summer destinations.) Still, you want a path that welcomes and pulls you into the garden—practical, yes, but attractive, too.

Straight vs. Winding Paths
The great tug between formal and informal gardening styles that was waged by theorists in both Europe and America over a period spanning two centuries was symbolized during that time, it seems, by the shape of the garden path. Eighteenth-century designers of formal gardens viewed the straight line as an extension of architecture into landscape, an organizing axis around which a garden might be

BAMBOO STRIPS SET IN A CONCRETE PATH

Straight lines spell autocracy, of which most European gardens are an expression, and their course points to intellectual decay, which soon develops a prison from which the mind can never escape.

Jens Jensen, from *Jens Jensen: Maker of Natural Parks and Gardens* by Robert Grese[6] planned. Proponents of "landscape" gardening, on the other hand, in reaction to what they perceived as tokens of insufferable rigidity and arrogance, regarded straight walkways as aberrations in nature.

We live in different times and feel free to integrate formal structure into very informal settings if we choose, and vice versa. Still, in my own garden, I want pathways that are sympathetic to the feeling of the whole, and different pathway lines *do* offer different experiences.

The curving or straight line of a path affects both function and mood in a garden. If you want a cozy, loose look, a meandering path will serve you well. It allows for surprises as you round a curve and permits new vantage points at different moments in the journey. While a straight path may have a large urn as a focal point at its end, a curving path allows you to create ornamental focal points in several places, depending on the size of your property. By planting flowering trees or shrubs inside the curves of a path, you draw the stroller's eyes and feet to the next bend.

Straight paths, while often associated with the strict geometry of formal gardens, can be wonderfully informal when they are set in a relaxed cottage or kitchen garden and made with less formal materials. The straightness of the line may be the only organizing visual element in an exuberant plant display, and may have the happy effect of providing calm in an otherwise chaotic picture.

The straight path sometimes provides an axis around which the remainder of the garden can be planned. Just as formal garden designers have connected house to garden with long lines that emanate from a doorway or window, you can use this organizing principle in your own backyard. And by terminating a straight path with a bench, you accomplish two things: You give visual focus as you move along the path or as you view it from your terrace, and you also provide seating for a view looking back at the house. In short, a path's straightness or curvy shape will be decided by its purpose and the mood of your garden.

A path will lie hard in the landscape if it is mortared, and for that reason I tend to prefer walkways that are set in sand. Shape, texture, and color of the paving materials decide whether a path looks soft or hard, dressed up or dressed down. Crazy paving—irregular stone shapes pieced together—is as homey as a quilt, while granite rectangles, neatly adjoined, work as a formal surface.

Spacing
The space you leave between stones affects the walk's formality: squeeze them together and you've got a proper-looking walkway; loosen them up, leaving space for living green fillers, and you've got a softer, more casual look. (Plant herbs, mosses, low-growing sedums, or grass in the cracks.) Green grass between path stones connects visually with the green of an adjacent lawn; it appears as all one piece of fabric. A graphic example of the power of spacing involves square-cut stone or concrete pavers. If you space the stone about two inches apart and set it diagonally into the turf, you create a dramatic green harlequin pattern that looks English-manor-formal-gone-slightly-decadent. A swipe with the lawn mower keeps it respectable.

Instead of stone or bricks, wooden rounds set into sand make an unusual path through the lawn.

Opposite: A crazy-quilt of brick and stone covers a terrace and meanders out into the garden. Artist Keelya Meadows used the same bold colors on walls and containers in the Berkeley, California, garden.

In contrast to the pathway to the right, this linear, uncluttered slate path could be used with almost any style of house that has a more minimalist style of garden.

This natural-looking stone path is charmingly planted with forget-me-nots, ferns, primula, and pachysandra. The wild, loose feeling is suitable for a country garden.

You don't need to set the stones diagonally to achieve a lovely pattern. The stones can be square or rectangular or a mix of both, and arranged straight across the length of a curving or straight path.

Style is about how a thing looks and *feels.* Japanese gardeners have raised pathmaking to an art form not only by attending to the shape and placement of stepping-stones but to the rhythm of one's footfalls upon them. Smaller stones may be arranged to slow down the stroller, while larger ones provide a resting point from which to view a garden feature. There's no more inspiring source for planning a stone path than a supply of Japanese gardening books. The simple, graphic elegance of these patterns—part of a deeply symbolic garden design philosophy—may inspire a path solution for your modern or rustic setting.

In my own landscape, I want my paths to feel as if they're a part of the ground, to recede rather than jump at me. I want the color and texture of the path to be neutral and soft so it makes a pleasant background for edging with plants, if I choose. And so I've used stone and gravel that is native to the eastern United States and looks completely at home on my land. I've found old bricks, aged to a fine patina, that absorb the light rather than reflect it. And I've made my paths straight, because I'd rather spend time in the rooms of my garden than in the hallways. But these are choices of style and are personal to every gardener.

General Advice on Paths

You have to look at the kinds of brick or stone native to your land and the color of your soil before choosing materials for landscaping your property. In the East, gray and tan gravels, red brick, and cobblestone look very natural, while white or bright reddish gravel doesn't. In the West, the earthy brownish-red of decomposed granite looks right at home.

When in doubt, I think the best approach is to drive around and look at what others have done in the surrounding area. I did this recently with a client when planning a driveway and we both found it enormously helpful to see big masses of different stonework already set into the landscape. Brick and stone yards will also have small sample sections of pavement already laid so you can see the whole effect.

Brick

Monochromatically and unnaturally orange-red, rectangular, and hard-looking, some new brick begs to be trampled upon, chipped away at with a pickax, and covered with dirt and moss. Not all new brick calls for abuse, though; some has already been distressed at the factory. If you prefer new brick but still want the look of the old stuff, with a little homework you can find some fair approximations that won't fight with plant colors. Look for handmade bricks or machine-made ones that have been tumbled for a weathered, organic feel. Tumbled bricks have been tossed in a barrel not unlike a concrete mixer to take off the hard edges.

You can also find handmade bricks that have been molded in tapered wooden forms. The clay is thrown into a sand-lined mold, scraped for a level edge, dried, then fired. The

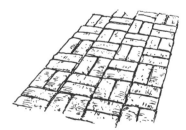

BASKETWEAVE BRICK PATH

HERRINGBONE BRICK PATH

result is a brick with irregularities and character. Colors will vary for handmade bricks, as they do in all brick.

Old Street Pavers

If you ever feel discouraged about the state of workmanship in today's building products, go to an antique brick salvage yard to have your spirits restored. "Guaranteed by God" is the response Phil Mumford of Chicago's Colonial Brick Company gives to customers who ask about the potential longevity of the old granite pavers stacked up outside his office. The hundred-year-old patina on Mumford's granite blocks and clay bricks makes them highly desirable to locals looking for the character and quality of earlier times.

The five-by-ten-inch granite blocks (some are four-by-four cubes) at the Colonial Brick Company have a wonderful texture with a fascinating history. During the 1880s and later, rough blocks of granite were hand hewn by farmers in their off season. They used hammers and chisels to texture the blocks, creating beautiful dressed surfaces for the humble street pavers.

Phil Mumford will be the first to tell you that if you're looking for the path of least resistance, antique pavers are not for you. Bricklayers hate them, he says, because they're not uniform. But the wonderful granite blocks, ranging in shades from speckled gray to pink, cost no more than concrete pavers and, with some love and attention, make charming garden paths.

What distinguishes Mumford's old clay bricks from new ones is not only their size (four by four by eight inches), which is two inches thicker and slightly larger than today's typical modular brick. Nor is it simply the color that differs, though the earthy browns and reds are a far cry from the jarring orange-red of many new bricks. No, it's something else that's hard to put your finger on, but clear when you finally see it—it's the texture of antique bricks that new ones can't approach. They're not flat, uniform, and identical, but pitted here and there, rough and irregular to the touch. Old street pavers were pressed twice in the manufacturing process—extruded first, then re-pressed to make them even more compact and durable. In that process the long sharp edges were rounded, and it's that subtle quality, along with color and about one hundred years of character building, that makes old street bricks a charming substitute for a concrete driveway, for exmple.

Here's Mumford's advice. First and foremost, you must use old bricks that have been reclaimed from streets and alleys, not building bricks, which are too porous and won't survive the freeze/thaw cycle. You'll know they're re-pressed antique pavers because they have raised letters or little bumps called "lugs."

The side that was originally up will be too worn to use, so you'll want to use the side of the brick that was previously laid facedown. Don't set the bricks in mortar. It hardens the appearance and will crack in a cold climate. You can set the bricks atop well-compacted earth and stone screening, which is a mix of gravel, clay, and stone dust. The absence of mortar also means the walk will be self-draining and will survive drastic temperature changes.

Above all, find someone who enjoys the challenge of working with old brick. That person may not be a

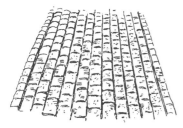

STRETCHER BOND BRICK PATH

bricklayer but a stonemason, someone who will not fight the bricks but will accept their idiosyncrasies and find a way to fit them together harmoniously.

Gravel

Ordering gravel without first seeing it is like ordering a beige rug—there are a million shades of it, and one man's tan is another man's gray. "Gravel" is a generic term, varying by region in its permutations. It is either crushed rock or rounded pebbles gathered from river and stream beds. Suppliers often have piles of white, gray, tan, and brown gravels, plus mixtures of all of the above, from which to choose. If possible, see it first installed in the landscape, and by all means pick out the color yourself. Once it has been laid, you may decide later, as I have, to mix in another color of gravel to soften the look. What's important is that you choose a color that blends subtly with the natural color of the earth where you live.

Gravel is an inexpensive, and potentially elegant, solution to the question of how to get from point A to point B. For anyone who has slushed through a gravel walkway laid too thickly with the stuff, though, the word "elegant" might not leap to mind. The trick in making such a path attractive is to avoid laying down too heavy a top layer of decorative gravel. The surface of a gravel path should feel hard, not mushy. The size of the gravel matters, too. James David, a landscape architect in Austin, Texas, insists on a thin top layer of rounded pea gravel three-eighths inch in size, for example.

It's also important to get the lines of your path correct,

whether straight or curving. (Too many tight curves will drive you wild while carrying groceries from car to back door.) Bricks, stone, or edging tiles will contribute to the cleanness of the path's lines in your landscape.

The gravel path connecting the kitchen garden with my house is laid on sloping ground. So the path is a series of straight level sections, which step down gradually to the garden. I've used long rectangles of limestone as steps, and these visually punctuate the mass of gravel. Over the path, there are hoops where honeysuckle grows in the summer.

Broken Concrete Paths

Southern California landscapers have found a way to recycle ugly parking lot concrete into useful and handsome garden hardscape materials. Called simply "broken concrete," chunks of cement are hauled from sidewalk and parking lot demolition sites and used to make paths, terraces, steps, and retaining walls.

The broken concrete is sometimes incorporated into hillside paths. What's amazing is that not only is it cheap, the concrete looks good—like stone, in fact—when its hard flat surface is broken up to reveal jagged edges and bumpy aggregate. The look can be aged with chemical stain that adds a slightly rusted appearance. Creeping thyme and Corsican mint don't mind cozying up to concrete as they do to stone; they thrive in broken concrete paths and retaining walls. And it's an alert eye that picks up the distinction between real stone and the concrete pretender.

Other concrete options exist out there. Precast, tinted, and interlocking pavers seem to be everywhere. While I

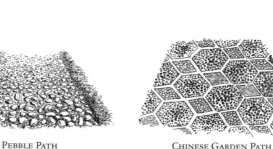

PEBBLE PATH

CHINESE GARDEN PATH

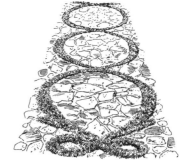

GRASS AND FIELDSTONE PATH

find many of these pavers terrific for commercial settings, I have yet to be convinced that they work well in a residential landscape. One exception that comes to mind is the gray-colored tumbled concrete paver that imitates the look of Belgian block stone. Loosely spaced and interplanted with green and growing life, these pavers can be softened. By and large, though, I prefer the organic materials: bricks, stone, and wood.

Grass Paths
There are grassy areas around my gardens that were once mown regularly. Our eyes have been trained to admire clipped lawns, but I find more beauty now in simple mown grass paths leading to the summer destinations that require them. The taller grass is filled with naturalized daffodils.

Grass pathmaking is a form of gardening in itself when one has a large property. Two Midwestern designers discovered this when they made the leap from city to country living.

CHARLOTTE AND DANIEL'S GARDENS
Charlotte Peters and Daniel Ward were garden designers on Chicago's affluent north shore before they pulled up roots and moved their garden ornament business to a one-hundred-acre farm called Longshadow Gardens at the southern tip of Illinois.

Accustomed to designing and installing gardens for suburban properties of much less acreage, the couple found that the farm's rolling hills, bluffs, meadows, and woodlands suggested new gardening possibilities.

Merging their passion for grand gardens and garden ornament with the special features of the farm's landscape, they created a series of "destination gardens" atop hills and deep in the woods.

Charlotte and Daniel chose spots most worthy of frequent visits and cut paths or vistas to those locations, then groomed those spaces where needed, removing saplings and brush to allow long views deep into woodland spaces, and pruning trees to lovelier shapes. Once the sweaty clearing work was done, they embarked on the equally sweaty but fun part—placing ornaments from their impressive collection to decorate those rooms. They carried heavy planters and statues down the steep wooded slopes by wheelbarrow, tractor, cart, and slings.

Their first path runs through a hayfield to a four-foot-high formal stone urn with lid. Beyond the urn, the path continues to a weathered bench where a visitor takes in a thirty-mile view that includes seven layers of receding hills covered with orchards, vineyards, and forests.

Another path invites the stroller through a woodland area, where columbines, trout lilies, Dutchman's breeches, and ferns grow densely on the rock outcroppings in spring. In a picturesque clearing, they have placed a blue bench near an osage orange tree. In early fall, when the six-inch lime-green hedge apples appear on the tree, their color plays off the blue of the bench and the gold of the leaves. Nearby, two fat Gertrude Jekyll–style containers filled with boxwood and ivy, which can overwinter in the mild southern Illinois climate, complete the vignette.

The considerable task of managing a hundred acres

STONE AND PEBBLE PATH

A natural path can be made by mowing a graceful curve through a field of summer flowers or grass.

opened their eyes to the value of pathmaking as a form of gardening. "It's an amazing opportunity to play with the native environment and garden ornament," says Daniel. "Nearly every style of urn we make has found a perfect home in one of the niches in the woods."

EDGING

Show me a garden formulated to its smallest detail and I'll show you a frustrated gardener. Nature has a way of changing our best-laid plans, and it's the confident gardener who learns from accidents and values serendipity. While the alchemilla may romp over the border and the cleome may sprout from terrace cracks, if there's a strong structural underpinning beneath the green chaos of summer, the picture still holds together. Edging helps make that happen.

Edging material around a bed makes a harder, more precise line, though, and you have to decide if you want a severe line. Perhaps the feeling you're seeking is very soft, in which case you won't edge, or you'll use organic materials that disappear, like stone, rather than stylized terra-cotta tiles to outline a border.

The value of edging is that it cuts down on maintenance, particularly where lawn and border meet. A row of flat bricks, stones, or tiles creates a mowing edge that permits the mower wheel to move along it and eliminates the extra work of trimming shaggy grass by hand.

Victorians used edging tiles because they bedded out plants, often in the middle of a lawn, and they needed a precise line for that effect. There are many reproductions

now of those Victorian edgers, including terra-cotta rope and poured stone basketweave tiles. These can make charming borders in kitchen gardens especially.

For a rustic feel, a wonderful look is achieved by taking branches of the red-twigged dogwood (or other shrub branches) and bending them to make a line of natural-looking hoops. Also wonderfully rustic are six- to eight-inch-high stones surrounding beds in a kitchen garden.

PARTERRES

Somewhere between the edge and the hedge falls the dwarf enclosure called the parterre. From the French *par terre*, meaning "on the ground," parterres are beds that are often surrounded by boxwood, and function as decorative divisions within formal gardens. In historic French gardens, parterres were arranged symmetrically in relation to a central axis. Sometimes a boxwood border contained complex scrollwork designs in trimmed grass that resembled embroidery patterns. These *parterres en broderie* were meant to be viewed from a terrace or window above so as to take in the overall pattern.[7]

Similar to Italian and French parterre gardens are traditional English knot gardens, which also employed low-growing edgings and interior interwoven knotlike lines of herbs. The spaces were then filled with colored gravels, or plants, or even coal dust.

Early Colonial settlers brought cuttings of box from the Old World and lovingly transplanted them, surely as reminders of the homes they had left behind. The basic dwarf boxwood hedge was present as a garden division at

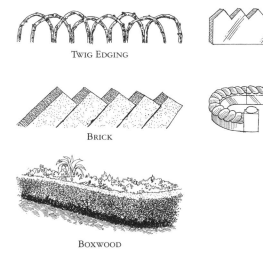

TWIG EDGING

TILE

BRICK

ROPEWORK

BOXWOOD

the Williamsburg settlement and still works for American gardeners today. It's a formal organizing device, but one that allows you to fill the rectangles, diamonds, and squares informally with vegetables and near-chaotic bouquets of flowers and herbs, if you choose. Parterres frame the picture and keep it looking neat.

THE LAWN

I like to think of the lawn as a green filler piece in a multicolored quilt. It's often a necessary piece (children *need* play areas), and it can be calming to look at. The contrast of the lawn's green simplicity makes the remainder of the quilt all the more brilliant.

And grass lawns can be particularly lovely as ground covers when they emphasize the natural undulations of a sweeping landscape. Designer Jack Lenor Larsen, for example, has used grass to blanket a "bowl" of earth in his garden. The sculptural medium is the earth, and the grass is its finish.

But grass lawns have become the end point for many homeowners, the prevailing metaphor for what passes as nature around our homes. That's unfortunate. Unlike the English aristocracy whose estate lawns inspired us, we have neither the weather nor the help, in most cases, to live up to the ideal of jewel-green carpets surrounding our castles.

When I started out planning my property, I wanted the most beautiful lawn and the biggest roses and whatever it took I was willing to do. But I am a changed gardener since those days. I have learned enough to know that the trade-off for a perfect lawn is the loss of other pleasures, among

them visiting birds and butterflies and clean groundwater. Why sacrifice those necessities for the sake of an aesthetic? No fashion is worth that price. Frederick Law Olmsted, the designer of New York's Central Park and one of America's greatest landscape planners, was a great proponent of open, grassy, parklike residential spaces—but I'd stake my life on the belief that, if he were alive today, he wouldn't put chemicals on his lawn. He loved nature too much.

I don't feel the need to have a perfect green carpet anymore, and because I live in the country, it's not a difficult issue for me. I haven't given up a lawn; I'm just content with a lawn that performs at about seventy percent of its previous, chemically enhanced capacity.

I realize, however, that in suburbs where the great green carpet connects communities, it's a more complicated problem, almost a political issue. If I lived in a place where lawns adjoin one another, I would find a way to shrink the space devoted strictly to grass, turn over more space to ground cover, and make the remaining lawn work as a plain, unpatterned contrast to more interesting plantings.

GROUND COVER

Traditionally we think of ground cover as a problem solver, a hardworking and low-maintenance substitute for grass, particularly in shade. And there's no question that it's a wonderful troubleshooter.

When ground cover is used effectively, however, it can become the connective tissue that gives visual continuity to a design in much the same way a rug or carpet does inside. I often use a neutral rug, such as wheat-colored sisal, to

The chief beauty of a lawn . . . lies in the contour of the land, the gracious curve and sweep of the surface, the play of shadows which great trees throw on the grass at their feet, excellences for which a lawn twenty by fifty feet gives little room.

Frances Duncan, *The Joyous Art of Gardening,* 1917[8]

help pull together a number of different sitting areas, furniture styles, and fabric patterns into one whole composition. Ground cover works in the same way. You can shape it so that its mass and color connects and unifies disparate elements—a tree here and a bed there—that are unrelated without it.

In a small garden, one kind of ground cover works best to achieve this effect. There's nothing more beautiful than walking through a path of ivy—just one kind of ivy. But little splats of different ground covers confuse the issue.

In a larger space, though, one can use ground covers to paint with abandon, brushing in sweeps of color that make the garden floor the focus of your room the way a beautiful Aubusson carpet does in a great hall. Vinca planted under scattered trees can connect them in an interesting way. An individual tree underplanted with a square of ajuga can enhance the beauty of the tree.

Chapter Seven:
The Roof Overhead

You think of the possibility of lying on stone,
Among fern fronds, and waiting
For the stars to find you.
The stars would not be astonished
To catch a glimpse of the form through interstices
Of leaves now black as enameled tin.
Nothing astounds the stars.
They have long lived.
And you are not the first
To come to such a place
  seeking the most difficult knowledge.

Robert Penn Warren, "The Place"[1]

When I was a child, I had a favorite spot in my aunt's garden where I could hide and play house. It was a stand of bamboo through which my aunt had cut a path and made a sort of interior room. She had placed a small table and chairs there, and I could have a tea party with friends or dolls or dogs, depending on who was available. A dappled light played over the little room, and when I looked up I could see the sky. It was the most delicious place for a child, I now realize, because it met that very primitive need we all have to feel cozy and safe, yet connected to the earth and sky.

In that private spot, bamboo canopy provided a roof overhead; in our grown-up gardens, it could be any tree that gives us the same feeling. Tree canopy completes the sense of partial enclosure that starts with the walls placed around the outdoor room. Trees regulate the amount of sunlight and shade that fill the garden room. And equally importantly, tall trees, like grand ornaments, pull our eyes up from our habitual gaze downward in the garden.

Think of every cathedral or lobby you've ever walked into that caused you to take in your breath. There's a great sense of volume. Outside, the sky is so vast we tend to ignore it in our gardens, focusing our eyes down at plants instead. But majestic old trees, or even smaller ornamental ones, provide a comfortable scale for us on so vast a canvas. They visually pull the sky into our garden landscapes.

Branches and leaves place form and contrasting color against the great blue backdrop. And whether it's the tracery of black twigs in winter, the chartreuse of new leaves in spring, the full green boughs of summer, or fall's

Palm trees scattered across the lawn form a strong vertical element on this property, and the sunlight filtering through the fronds creates a beautiful pattern on the ground.

Next page: Live oaks and magnolias form a canopy over a New Orleans garden.

blazing bursts of yellow, orange, and red trees against the sky cause us to catch our breath and say, "Look at that. Isn't it beautiful?"

But what about those places where the sky *is* the view, places with "big sky," like Montana? I'm not sure why the sky of Montana appears to be so much vaster than elsewhere. Perhaps it is the unbroken vistas and the mountains in the distance. All I can say is that I was properly awed and humbled by the endless heavens when I visited there.

Sky is to Montana what the Pacific Ocean is to California: a magnificent wonder. It is a wonder, however, with which no garden can compete. And that's why, especially in places like Montana, if I purchased a new house my first act of ownership, if there were no canopy, would be to plant the biggest trees I could afford. Because no garden plants can ever measure up to such a view of the sky. In order to establish a more intimate relationship to my plants, I'd need a roof overhead.

This thinking applies to all those new houses across America that have been plunked down in the middle of a field with nary a tree in sight, the potential canopy having been removed in years past for agricultural reasons, or more recently eliminated by a bulldozer during construction. Rather than circling such a house with foundation plantings, I'd blow the landscaping budget in a wink on big trees that would anchor the house to the land.

In vast properties especially, the sky is a very important visual element in certain parts of the garden. But those areas will be made more special if other parts of the garden are canopied. You will feel a change of mood and a change

A planting of eucalyptus in Dick Martin's garden creates a room with the tree canopy as its ceiling.

Birch trees planted in parallel form a memorable gallery connecting one open space to another.

A corridor cuts through the woods, drawing the visitor to an urn lit by the sun.

Weeping willows form a cool sanctuary in the garden.

in the feeling of space by going from the protected shelter of a canopy to the wide-open sky, which has no limits, and thus no intimacy. This is true whether you create shade with trees or pergolas. You feel a dramatic difference progressing through the garden because you've changed the roof overhead, if only for a moment.

LIGHT AND SHADE

Ideally, one would have room enough and trees enough for full sun, dappled shade, and full shade when you want it. There's such pleasure in the contrast of moving from shade to sun, or observing a sunny garden from a shady spot. Not every gardener is gifted with such light patterns, though. For every treeless garden naked to the sky, there is another somewhere so shaded by old tree canopy as to make gardening seem mere fantasy.

When I first bought my home, my garden was overpowered by too much canopy from the maples, but by selectively thinning out the trees I have increased the light under those trees by about fifty percent. I also continually work with a wonderful old hawthorn—thinning and pruning it—to have a prettier shape and less density in terms of shade.

Dappled shade is the best of all possible worlds in my view, and there are a number of trees that will accommodate you with just such an effect. Birches and dogwoods, for example, have lacy, airy forms.

If you have existing canopy that creates deep shade, you can discuss doing some thinning with a tree expert. Dappled shade may be only a few critical cuts away.

Even if you have a glorious canopy presently, it makes sense to plant a young tree or two to replace the older ones that will eventually die. You may live to appreciate your own forethought when you find the tree in a mature state when you need it. Or today's tree-planting gesture may simply be a gift to some future gardener who occupies your piece of the earth.

A PRIVATE ROOM IN THE TREES

Small fruit trees make quick cover, creating the most intimate spaces when they are planted and pruned for shelter. I've seen this done with apple trees. Four of them had been planted in a grid, one tree at each corner, then pruned to form a canopy over a sitting area. Below the leafy bower was a rough square of scattered stones, which served as a platform for a small stone table and a couple of metal chairs. Green grass poked up from the cracks between stones. It was the most simple but delicious of gardens.

Apple trees are somehow archetypal, but other trees will do. The redbud or cherry tree will make such a vignette. What could be nicer than walking along a mowed path in a sunny field to get to such a cool little shelter?

Shrubs will lend themselves to this purpose, as well. My dear friend, landscaper Nancy McCabe, has many delightful spots in her garden but one of my favorites is a small grove of sumac, pruned to form a little hallway that leads you to her chicken house. The sumac, regarded in some parts as a weedy interloper, has been elegantly groomed in Nancy's garden. Underplanted with hellebores, the sumacs provide filtered shade in summer, brilliant red

Comfort me with apples . . .
Song of Solomon, 2:5

THE ROOF OVERHEAD

One is always drawn to a shady spot on a hot day, and this canopy of **Cornus** *florida (dogwood) makes an especially inviting place to stroll.*

color in fall, and serve as a wonderful destination on a garden walk.

One other aspect that tree form provides is the silhouette against the sky. At Innisfree, the Millbrook, New York, garden I described earlier, there are willow trees growing next to a large pond. What is so unusual about the willows is that they have been pruned against type (and personality) —a process called "pollarding" (see page 41). Instead of dripping to the ground, their boughs are clipped at midtrunk level. The trees appear to be gay green parasols lining the edge of the water.

On one visit to the garden, the willows made so unexpected a sight that it took me a moment to identify them. They create a powerfully graphic form against the sky. Palm trees work in the same way, punctuating the vast sky with their bursts of dark fronds.

Planning your tree canopy should be one of the first items that you deal with on your property. If you are lacking trees, figure out where you want them—this is a big step, so plan carefully. Plant your trees first even though it may be the most expensive thing you do, as you willl have to wait some time for them to mature. But it is a short time to wait for something so marvelous.

A metal arbor placed over a curved stone wall in this garden at Kykuit, the Rockefeller estate in New York's Hudson Valley, creates a little room furnished with stone toadstools, perfect for picnic lunches.

CHAPTER EIGHT: PASSAGEWAYS

The best way out is always through.

Robert Frost, "A Servant to Servants," 1914[1]

Modern-day gardeners could take a few clues from nineteenth-century suitors on the subject of gates. A gentleman courting a lady viewed the garden gate as an opportunity for romance, for a bold statement, or at least for a bit of fun. I think they were on to something.

Architectural elements at the garden entry provide opportunities to create interest. A whimsical red metal gate, a white lattice arbor with inset benches, a rustic pergola leading to a door—all these set the mood for the experience to come.

There's a language to the garden entry, too. A high stockade gate set in a fence discourages visitors, while a low wooden gate welcomes them. A black iron gate between two brick columns is a formal threshold; remove the gate, and the entry remains dignified but a bit more relaxed. A tunnel formed by arching hoops pulls you in.

The entryway introduces the garden, frames your first view of it, and creates a sense of anticipation. Gates, arbors, pergolas, and hoops are the doors and hallways of discovery—they move the feet and the eyes across the threshold or through a tunnellike passage into the open space of the garden. And once inside, looking back at the entry offers its own pleasures when the entry's form is sculptural or climbing vines add vertical color and interest.

GATES

There are practical considerations in choosing a gate for an enclosure, among them the need to keep children and pets in, and deer out, of a garden. But gates work as focal points and decorative touches, too, whether open or closed.

Visitors are lured through a hallway of yews at Filoli, in Woodside, California.

Imagine a large doorway into a living room. Now picture the same frame with open French doors attached to it. Which do you prefer? Even if they are never closed, I prefer the doors to be there. Why? I think it has to do with the possibility of enclosure, and the potential for privacy and security if I want it.

Doors add architectural detail to a room, indoors or out. And just as you would repeat the period and style of a particular door throughout your house, you can reiterate an element of your house's architecture in your garden gate. If you have a Carpenter Gothic–style house, for example, with a distinctive arched door, you can repeat the form in your gate. The front door will be heavier and larger and the gate will be lighter, and perhaps a different color. But the repetition will connect the house and garden beautifully, especially if the two are lined up on the same axis.

You can also have fun with color, form and pattern when choosing a gate. While you wouldn't necessarily want a red or chartreuse or yellow fence, a gate in one of those hues, set into a weathered fence, could be quirky yet smashing in the right setting. Or tie it in with the color palette of the stone in the garden for a particularly attractive look.

Consider dressing up a simple wooden picket fence with a chinoiserie-patterned gate. The simplicity of the lines of chinoiserie fretwork is compatible with both traditional and contemporary houses. Or scout out an old wood or iron gate at a salvage yard. A wooden gate, weathered to a fine patina, may spark the design for the fence. By choosing the gate first, you can build the fence the appropriate height, and not have to try to make a gate fit into the existing enclosure.

Come into the garden, Maud,
For the black bat, night, has flown,
Come into the garden, Maud,
I am here at the gate alone.
Alfred Lord Tennyson, "Maud," 1855[2]

IRON GATE AND BRICK PIERS

WOODEN GATE AND ARBOR

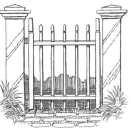

PICKET GATE

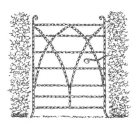

COUNTRY IRON GATE

FORMAL IRON GATE

129

Pots placed in a row on a garden wall transform it into living architecture. The terra rossa pots, filled with plumbagos, can be moved inside for the winter months.

Previous page: The lovely, Japanese-inspired moon gate in a soft pink stucco wall in the Rockefellers' Maine garden creates not only a doorway but a striking frame for the Buddha figure beyond.

PIERS AND COLUMNS

Piers are a wonderful way to mark a threshold, and while the idea of building a garden wall may be a bit daunting, brick piers may fall within your budget. You can set a pair of piers into a hedge, top the coping with stone baskets or ball finials, and garner some of the sense of permanence one feels with a masonry wall. A simple wooden gate set within piers in a hedge adds great charm, while a metal gate opens up the view.

Piers should be consistent with the house's material—whether it's brick or poured concrete or cinder block. They should approximate the height of the hedge rather than tower awkwardly above it. The coping, or cap, at the top of a pier is yet another opportunity to subtly pull some design element of the house out into the garden.

Ornamental iron newel posts, four-sided and columnar in shape, offer a lighter variation on the masonry pier theme. Newel posts twelve inches square and up are substantial enough to set within the opening of a hedge. Top them with iron balls or acorn finials, add a gate, and you have a look the most refined Victorian would envy. New iron gates and newel posts are still made by foundries using the same designs that charmed homeowners a hundred years ago.

I like piers as threshold markers not only at the garden perimeter but also at points of transition. Simple wood piers, set beside a path at the end of a lawn and the beginning of a meadow, lead the eyes to that passageway and help express the opening. A wonderfully elegant look can also be achieved at thresholds by placing two columns side by side and topping each with a cornice.

PERGOLAS AND ARBORS

Surely I am no different than generations of gardeners before me: The moment I knew what a pergola was, I wanted one desperately. Walking beneath the rustic covered walkway at Old Westbury Gardens in Long Island, I fell under its spell, and knew then that a pergola eventually would find its way into my garden.

There's a romantic sense of privacy and a delightful contrast of cool shade to hot sun within a vine-covered pergola. In Italy, in a culture that enjoys outdoor living, pergolas have long been used to support grape vines and provide relief from the intense midday heat.

Pergolas are covered walkways constructed of posts or columns and overhead trelliswork or beams. Sometimes they connect two buildings, creating wonderful green cover from a garage to a house, for example. Because they are typically located over walks, pergolas are similar to interior hallways: They are meant to lead somewhere, though they become rooms, too, when they're furnished. In fact, a pergola can be a garden unto itself. Cover it with wonderful vines, pull a table and some chairs under it, and surround yourself with fragrant potted standards.

Some people use the terms "arbor" and "pergola" interchangeably, and I must admit, I'm one of them. The more permutations one sees of each, the fuzzier the distinction becomes. "Arbor" is the broader term, taking in many green-covered shelters, including the leafy niches created by trees pruned to arch overhead. Man-made arbors are airy concoctions of open metal or wood (often lattice) work. They include shallow trellis arches primarily

BRICK PIER   CEMENT PIER   VICTORIAN PIER

A metal arbor covered in grapes could be at home in almost any garden. This one gives respite from the sun and leads a visitor down the stone path to yet another garden room beyond.

A great stylized passageway is created by this chinoiserie-inspired wooden pergola in a garden in Annapolis, Maryland. Notice the unusual plum-colored wood with chartreuse yellow laburnum.

Opposite: Plainly constructed of cedar poles, Ryan Gainey's pergola adds rustic, charmed form to his Atlanta garden.

intended for vine support, or larger open-air destinations furnished with benches and tables.

Whatever shape your arbor or pergola takes, if it's to be near your dwelling, look to the lines and mood of your house for design direction. A glass and steel home may call for a spare steel pergola, for example. I recall a midwestern white stucco house with a distinctive eyebrow shape in the portico over the front door and on top of the dormer windows. The homeowner had built a wonderful high lattice fence surrounding the garden. Over the gate, I noticed, the arbor arched like an eyebrow. It was a small architectural reference, just a wink back at the house, but it connected the garden to the house beautifully.

A pergola (or is it an arbor?) eventually did come to rest at the edge of my kitchen garden, forming a part of the enclosure. More kin to the barn than to my house, it is a rustic invention of locust trees harvested from the woods nearby and nailed together with the bark still on. Covered with honeysuckle and morning glories in summer and furnished with an old bench and some potted heliotrope, it is the spot in which I am most likely to find a missing guest relaxing, and breathing deeply.

NATURAL OPENINGS

Some of the most breathtaking openings are created entirely with living plants. Nature offers threshold markers of its own—two strong trees beside a woodland path entrance, for example—and your task may simply be to clear away brush and trees that confuse the message.

Or you can plant your own living threshold markers. I have a small woodland area on my property that I have been working with recently. I planted two white birches at the point at which you leave the kitchen garden and walk into the woods. The birches stand out against the green background and frame the passage; they pull you in and encourage you to proceed. The best gardens incorporate openings that entice you, yet don't reveal what's up ahead.

You can also use natural arches as frames for a view. One wonderful example that comes to mind is a church where two large redbuds flank a sidewalk leading to the church's heavy wooden doors. They mirror the lines of the doors and make a breathtaking fuchsia frame in springtime.

Hallways

Perhaps the most photographed garden feature in history is Rosemary Verey's laburnum walk at Barnsley House in England. And for good reason. The walk makes an extraordinary picture in spring, with a carpet of purple alliums blooming beneath yellow laburnum blossoms.

The unexpected discovery I made when I visited her garden, however, was how small a plot of land it really is, and how great a gardening impact she has made there. The laburnum walk is indeed a central focus of the garden, but it also works as a central axial hallway which creates rooms on either side of it. The laburnum "walls" also work as backdrops. In each garden room, later-blooming annuals and perennials are planted against the laburnum wall; outside the opposite laburnum wall one finds irises. And because the garden has such strong structure, it is beautiful even when few flowers are blooming.

I remember a wide, low arbor. . . . Underfoot was a brick path edged with violets, overhead were grape-vines, and on each side, half under the arbor and half outside, were peonies and irises. No one thought of calling it a pergola. It was merely the way to the kitchen-garden.

Frances Duncan, *The Joyous Art of Gardening,* 1917[3]

A pergola must not be a mean, light-built affair. It should be of good proportions and substantial materials. It need not be made with brick or marble pillars; natural tree trunks of good size serve as well. . . . A pergola may have a dilapidated Present and be endurable; but it should show evidences of a substantial Past.

Alice Morse Earle, *Old Time Gardens*, 1901[4]

Simple stucco columns with metal hoops supporting clematis provide not only a serene vista but a cool shaded walk through the garden.

An arched, vine-covered trellis provides an intimate, roofed passageway lined with seats at the Villa d'Este in Tivoli, Italy.

Hallways can also be made by erecting metal hoops and covering them with vines. I have recently done this over the gravel pathway from my house to the kitchen garden. It's still early to see the full effect, but in its second season, honeysuckle is gradually making its way up and over the arches. Stand at the edge of the house where the tunnel line begins and you see at its end the rustic gate of the kitchen garden. Turn around and look back at that point, and you will see a large stone urn planted with one strong agave.

ALLÉES

The alley or French *allée* is an avenue or hallway, depending on its scale, created by planting trees or shrubs in parallel lines along a walkway. It is a convention that's found in formal English, Dutch, French, and Italian gardens. Renaissance gardeners used *allées* to emphasize linear perspective, at that time a revolutionary development in art, architecture, and garden design.

Allées have been used in many formal American gardens. At Filoli in Woodside, California, an extraordinary *allée* of Irish yews works as a strong focal point in the formal garden. The approach was also adapted with native plant material early in this century by the great midwestern landscaper Jens Jensen, who is most frequently associated with naturalistic park design.

In 1916, Jens Jensen was invited to design the Shakespeare Garden at Northwestern University in Evanston, Illinois, to honor the three-hundredth anniversary of the bard's death. Inspired by Francis Bacon's 1625 essay "Of Gardens," in which the author detailed the many "alleys" one would find in his ideal garden, Jensen Americanized the idea by using native hawthorn trees around a rectangular rather than a square garden.

Jensen obtained 450 hawthorn (*Crataegus crus-galli*) seedlings, shipped them to France to be nurtured for five years, then planted them as one continuous *allée* running the entire perimeter of the central garden. The hawthorns created shady hallways, plus a privacy enclosure and backdrop for the sunny interior garden. Jensen left openings in the *allée* (a circular bench on one end, a statue of Shakespeare on the other) and cut openings on the two remaining sides so that modern-day strollers could use the *allée* as earlier visitors might have—a shady tunnel from which to view bright floral pictures of the interior garden.

Today, the central garden spills over with pansies, marigolds, stock, pinks, lilies, roses, and herbs—plants mentioned by Shakespeare in his plays and sonnets. But it's the hawthorn *allée,* now over eighty years old, that is the most stunning aspect of the garden.

I believe the idea could be adapted to a typical square or rectangular backyard. Anita Philipsborn, the Shakespeare Garden's cochairman, suggests using other types of hawthorns, since *Crataegus crus-galli* is extremely thorny and ill-suited for a garden frequented by children. She estimates that it took eight years for the hawthorns to reach mature size, and points out that the inner row of Jensen's *allée* is trimmed to a height of eight feet while the outer row is kept at ten feet. This allows the viewer standing at the center of the garden to perceive that the lush green row of trees is not only a hedge, but in fact a tunnel.

The garden is best to be square, encompassed on all the four sides with a stately arched hedge.

Francis Bacon, "Of Gardens," 1625[5]

III

FURNISHING THE GARDEN

CHAPTER NINE: CONTAINERS

{Le Nôtre} has left standing a little dark wood which is very pleasing; and next comes a little wood of oranges in great tubs: you can stroll in this wood which has shady avenues, and there are hedges on both sides cut breast high, so as to conceal the tubs, and these are full of tuberoses, roses, jasmine and pinks. This novelty is certainly the prettiest, most surprising and ravishing that one could imagine, and the little wood is greatly liked.

Madame de Sévigné on visiting André Le Nôtre's garden at Versailles in 1675[1]

At the end of a long gray winter, few mercies are more tender than the sight of a spring flower pot. It may be a container of yellow daffodils on a fire escape or lavender pansies spilling from a stone urn that last week was filled with snow. Whatever the flower, those blooms bobbing in the chill air are sweet relief to winter-weary passersby. And for the frustrated gardener, they are both an act of faith and statement of intent: Damn the weather, full speed ahead.

Let's face it. Container gardening is better than therapy for ending the winter blues. Its gratifications are certainly more immediate. What could be easier (or healthier) than plopping whatever the nursery is offering into a terra-cotta pot and creating a bouquet that cozies up the steps one day and flanks the garden gate the next?

Most of us delight in filling urns, window boxes, even old shoes with flowers and greenery. Yet containers often end up in supporting roles in our gardens. They play second fiddle to the perennial border, which, despite its difficult temperament, usually gets the starring role. I think the humble container deserves another audition.

CONTAINED STRUCTURE

Consider this: Some of history's great gardeners used containers as structural elements in their gardens. Around 1400 B.C., the Egyptians, the world's earliest pleasure garden stylists, highlighted their formal rectilinear gardens by placing at regular intervals large earthenware vases planted with trees and shrubs.[2] André Le Nôtre, the brilliant seventeenth-century designer who created Versailles for Louis XIV, used ornately decorated urns on

Terra-cotta containers of helichrysum and santolina soften and accentuate my stone steps.

pedestals to draw the visitor's eye down the garden's long avenues. He also created movable forests of fruit trees using wood containers. The Versailles box, today used by gardeners the world over, originated as a method to contain and transport orange trees in and out of the orangery at the great French garden.

While no one gardens in the grand manner of the pharaohs or Louis XIV today, there are lessons to be learned from their gardens, even for the most modest of our outdoor plans. We can use containers to define space, to direct the eye, and to stop the eye in our own backyards.

In my own garden I have found containers terrifically useful for creating garden rooms and emphasizing existing structure. For example, I've created a low "wall" with a row of identical terra-cotta pots placed atop a stone retaining wall. They mark the end of the lawn area and the beginning of the lower formal garden. The pots also alert unwary evening strollers who might otherwise topple over the edge without a visual warning.

As visitors walk down the stone steps set in the middle of the retaining wall and enter the symmetrical formal garden, two weeping pear trees in large pots frame their view of the reflecting pond and the arbor and path beyond it. In the distance, at the end of the vista, a large urn on a column serves as a focal point.

Containers aren't just for structuring formal settings, though. In the kitchen garden, I use terra-cotta pots with some of my favorite small plants—dianthus, auriculas, and pansies—elevated on wooden plant stands so I can see them easily. The containers add height and structure to an informal, exuberant planting scheme without intrusion.

Also in the kitchen garden, a lemon tree in a large pot serves as a focal point. Potted fuchsia and fragrant heliotrope standards, placed near a bench inside the garden's pergola, enhance the sense of yet another room within a room. I've found it's worth it to move those fruit trees and exotic plants too fragile to make it through a Connecticut winter into the greenhouse or to a sunny spot in my kitchen. For my efforts, I have been rewarded with the sweet summer fragrance of heliotrope in the dead of January.

Create a Wall

Before you think about what you'll plant in your containers, consider *where* your containers can effect the greatest impact in your garden.

A row of identical containers can be used to mark perimeters and define space within your garden. You can also create living walls by filling long wooden troughs with small trees. On a flagstone patio, in the absence of ground in which to plant, a row of arborvitae in wooden containers draws a green curtain of privacy.

The key to simulating a wall is using one long or several identical planters. On a terrace attached to a traditional house, consider a series of Versailles boxes filled with round boxwood. Or, if you have a modern house with a patio, place the boxwood in plain square containers.

Lead Guests In

Pots along a pathway welcome visitors and tell them where to go. A row of containers alternated with boxwood shrubs borders the brick path to my front door. A guest who arrives at the end of my driveway may find himself perplexed facing the side rather than the front entrance of my home. So the containers are there to nudge visitors toward the more formal front door. (This works quite well with newcomers, though the side door remains the entrance of choice among incorrigible old friends who ignore my traffic direction.)

When straight pathways are lined with pots, I prefer the same-sized pot be used with the same plant or similar plants. Gray-leaved plants such as sage and helichrysum create a nice effect. By using similarly colored plants, or one variety of scented geranium, for example, you establish a more precise line.

Mark a Doorway

A staircase lined with pots makes a charming front garden for any house and brings the eye to the entrance. March three or four identical pots filled with large fall mums up either side of your steps and you'll create an enticing passageway for arriving guests.

There's nothing more welcoming than a pair of containers on each side of a front door. Whether you choose formal, symmetrical spiral topiary evergreens or massed bouquets of fragrant mixed annuals, the containers warmly greet visitors and say, "Start Here." Containers placed beside garage doors soften the structure and pull it into the garden scheme.

You can mark a threshold between garden rooms or identify a transition with containers as well. A pair of containers at the end of a meadow's mown path formalize the entry into a woodland garden.

Connecting House and Garden: Soften Architecture, Add Detail

If you're planning a terrace or porch addition, consider integrating planters into the design. Frank Lloyd Wright wed his houses to the outdoors by building planters into and on top of walls. Wright's architectural drawings characteristically featured ivy spilling over a wall or large urns placed on low outer walls.

Wright used the *shape* of his containers as architectural detail. Wide, horizontal lips on stone planters echo the lines of some of his prairie houses. In other cases, the architect used a simple curving half-sphere to contrast with the straight clean lines of his buildings.

Sometimes in doing interiors I find that what a bland space needs is architectural detail—molding, perhaps, that was removed or never added in the first place. Think of the exterior wall of your house or garage as one of the walls of a garden room. Then add the details the blank slate craves.

Against a simple taupe-colored stucco house with sage green trim, for example, Nancy McCabe has placed two wooden boxes fitted with bamboo trellises painted the same color. In summer she grows climbing morning glories in the boxes. The planters lend architectural interest while the vines soften the austerity of a blank wall and integrate the house into the garden.

Hanging Gardens Emphasize Existing Lines

Hanging planters can enhance the architecture of a house

A Versailles box filled with morning glories climbing bamboo stakes makes a gracious welcome at a front door.

Perfectly placed stone pots mark the entrance to this knot garden, harmonizing beautifully with both the gray stone and gray plants.

by following its lines. On a long side veranda of a white frame house, for example, a series of identical large ferns hung at the same elevation makes a green hallway out of an ordinary porch. The trick with hanging containers is to obscure unattractive plastic baskets by choosing large enough plants, or using moss-filled wire baskets when appropriate. Avoid hanging the pots too high.

For a Victorian cottage with arching gingerbread at the porch corners, stagger containers to follow the curve. And hide unattractive wire hangers by overplanting the top of the porch with English ivy or grape. The effect is that of a lush and colorful swag framing a porch room.

Frame a Picture, Create a Focus

Large urns on pedestals are great for framing a vista. If you are lucky enough to have a view of mountains, ocean, meadows, or woodland beyond your garden or terrace, consider framing that view with containers. Place two large urns planted with trees or evergreens in a symmetrical arrangement at the edge of your terrace or lawn, framing a view the way you would a painting or photograph. Or you may use low containers with columnar evergreens to create a living frame.

Large pots and urns are great focal points, too, when elevated on stands and placed in the border, at the end of an *allée,* or on either end of a terrace.

John Rosselli has a wonderful hill behind his barn in the New Jersey countryside. In the field at the base of the hill he has placed a huge formal stone urn on a pedestal. Your eye is drawn to it immediately and then you notice the beautiful cedars scattered up the hill. That urn is completely unexpected and terrific as a focal point.

Compose with Pots

So much of garden design involves pulling together elements for a lovely visual composition. You may find that a large empty pot set amid tall flowers or grasses elevates a garden scene to art. Or you may want to use a subtle container planted with a shape that's needed in an otherwise perfect tableau.

Groups of pots massed together in a corner or on a terrace against a house create the illusion of a small flower garden when you arrange with form, texture, shape, and color in mind. In these groupings, pots will be more interesting if the shapes and sizes differ.

Lend Magic with Movable Color

I know a Midwest urban gardener, Medard Lange, who uses containers the way illusionists use top hats—to pull magic right out of them. On the terrace behind his brick row house, Med uses two cherub-decorated terra-cotta pots to anchor a glorious floral arch. The wide pots accommodate the sides of a soaring metal hoop that Med crafted from pipe. In summer, twined with white solanum, the arch makes a grand entrance into the formal garden below.

Med is especially savvy about color in the garden, since he's an accomplished florist. But when he returns home after a day of arranging brilliant flowers, he repairs to an almost monochromatic parterre garden. There, he says, he finds peace in the calmness of the green geometry.

This cast-concrete prairie-style planter makes a strong architectural statement as it sits at the edge of my reflecting pool holding an Acanthus mollis.

When he wants color in his urban oasis, Med uses containers to move it in and out. Some thirty-five years ago, when he laid out the garden's floor plan, he cleverly left room between the brick wall and the outer edge of the boxwood parterres. In that narrow space he places pots atop moss-covered columns to create a movable flower display.

Now, when the impulse hits him, Med dresses his basic green in the color that most interests him. When his business kept him from his garden until dusk, that color was the white of fragrant tuberoses and lilies, whites that glow in the darkness. Recently, he has chosen colorful azaleas and a variety of standards. Once, for a friend's wedding in his garden, he scattered rose petals over the brick paths and filled the green parterres with pots of lavender and blue hydrangeas. It was the perfect backdrop for the statuesque bride, who wore a rosebud garland Med had fashioned, with trailing streams of ivy for a veil.

Med also uses pots to encircle his English lead fountain with green garlands. He places containers of ivy near the base of it, then trains the ivy up and along wire swags around the dish of the fountain. Ivy garlands cover the brick garden walls, as well.

Med has known for years what so many gardeners come to understand—that containers can create atmosphere and drama and grandeur and whimsy in a garden.

OBJECTS OF DESIRE

At Treillage, garden containers are a significant part of our business. And with an excuse to scout out the most wonderful examples, my partner, John, and I have

A bold planting of phormium and grasses is enhanced by the placement of this large terra-cotta pitcher. The contrast of color and texture draws your eye to the corner of this garden.

STONE TROUGH WITH SUCCULENTS

indulged our passion for planters of all kinds.

Since we started Treillage in 1991, we've noticed that, along with a resurgence in gardening interest, pot-making is enjoying a comeback. I love the beauty and charm of handmade pots especially, and now stock them from all parts of the world, including Italy, France, the Netherlands, Mexico, Belgium, England, Spain, Portugal, and the United States. We carry lovely carved stone, lead, wood, and metal containers, as well as some convincing imitations, but the containers that I end up choosing for myself are, most often, made of terra-cotta.

In Praise of Baked Earth

There's something comforting about a terra-cotta pot. Beyond the pleasant feel and smell of terra-cotta, I find it reassuring that in a world wired with faxes and PC's, there are still craftsmen pulling clay from the earth, forming it with their hands, and baking it in the age-old fashion of the earliest potters.

During the first year of Treillage's operation, the search for great containers led John and me to the little Tuscan town of Impruneta, just outside of Florence. Impruneta is rarely mentioned in tourist guidebooks. Twenty minutes south of Florence, it is an architecturally unimpressive country cousin to the magnificent hometown of the Medicis. But Florence owes part of its grandeur to the tile makers and potters whose handiwork roofs and decorates that city today. For me, visiting Impruneta was akin to traveling to Mecca.

The first thing you notice about Impruneta is the dust.

In fact the whole town, covered with a heavy layer of pinkish grit, appears to be made of terra-cotta. Outside of long tin buildings, men sit at potting wheels molding the smooth clay that comes from the Tuscan hills around the town, the same clay the Etruscans used over two thousand years ago to make containers. Others work inside the sheds, rolling little balls into grape shapes and forming leaves with their hands. Pots of every shape and size surround the workers, embellished with the distinctive fruit designs, bouquets, lion masks, and della Robbia garlands that have decorated Italian pots for centuries.

With so many wonderful choices, placing an order was difficult that day, but we managed. Now we regularly stock Impruneta's terra-cotta for those gardeners who want a little piece of Italian earth in their American gardens.

I find the most beautiful Italian containers have a lovely pinkish tinge, unlike the ubiquitous factory-made orange ones we find in our garden centers. It is the oxidation of iron in the clay during the baking process that turns the pots a distinctive pink and earns them the name "terra rossa."[3]

ONE POT AT A TIME

Large, exquisitely decorated Italian terra-cotta pots do not come cheap. Terra-cotta shipped from foreign countries is sometimes costly because so much breakage occurs and because the shipping itself is expensive. It's not unusual for us to lose up to one-third of a shipment to breakage, despite the pot-maker's most careful packing. (In fact, the basement of Treillage is currently full of pots smashed in transit.)

Nonetheless, once you've developed a taste for the earthy

Moss Magic
You can make your pots look mossy and weathered by coating them with a yogurt mixture. In a blender, mix together moss with yogurt, buttermilk, or manure and some water. Using a paint brush, apply the mixture to the pots you want to age. Then place the pots in a cool shady spot and let the moss take over. Be sure to keep the pots damp to encourage moss growth. In the off season, avoid dry storage spots.

pink of an Italian pot, it's hard to go back to the mass-produced bright orange flower pots we're all familiar with. I continue to garden in the latter (all the while rubbing on dirt to tone them down), but each year I budget into my garden plan a couple of Italian terra-cotta containers.

Italy is not the only source for good terra-cotta, of course. I love the earthy oil jars made in Greece and Spain, either empty or with plants trailing over the sides. The English produce a vast array of elegant choices in their country potteries, though I find irresistible the simple longtoms—tall, narrow pots originally used by nineteenth-century nurserymen to grow long-rooted plants.

China now exports yellow-tinged terra-cotta that offers a nice, rustic-looking, and very inexpensive alternative to the machine-pressed orange terra-cotta we see so often. Also wonderful are the etched terra-cotta pots from Greece, glazed Portuguese pots, and those from Mexico, which are less ornate than the Italian but quite charming. And some of today's most exciting pottery emanates from the workshops of American potters who are producing distinctly original designs and elevating pot-making to an art form.

STONE
In the seventeenth and eighteenth centuries, stonecutters produced magnificent carved containers from quarried stone for the great gardens of Europe. And though the number of ornamental stone carvers has diminished dramatically, that doesn't mean you can't have a lovely stone trough in your garden. Many wonderful artificial stone containers in a wide range of traditional and modern designs are available in reconstituted limestone or the less expensive cast concrete. Recently I sold eight very large (four feet in diameter) but shallow cement dishes with spherical bottoms to a woman who was using them around her pool. Simple and sculptural, they work beautifully with her modern house.

When choosing a cast cement or stone container, look for examples that don't have obvious seams from molds or air bubbles that flaw the surface. Because reconstituted limestone is more porous than concrete, it can weather the freeze and thaw cycles of winter in northern climates. Before investing in a costly "stone" container that might crack during weather changes, it makes sense to consult a knowledgeable garden ornament dealer to learn what's "hardy" in your part of the world.

There are some fabulous fake containers out there that imitate stone but are made of fiberglass. These are great when authenticity is not an issue but storage space is. You can leave a fiberglass container outside through a Minnesota winter and still find it in one piece come May. Or you can move it around at your whim, unlike the real thing.

THE RIGHT CONTAINER FOR THE RIGHT SPOT
Choosing the right container and complementing it with the right plants is akin to creating a living still-life. When you select plant material for a composition, think like an artist. What style of container is appropriate for the spot you've chosen? Where will you place the container and how will you view it most often? What form and scale will the

IRON URN   TERRA-COTTA POT   FLAT IRON URN

Italian terra-cotta pots filled with heliotrope standards, gray-leafed santolina, and helichrysum line the paths of my kitchen garden.

A simple cast-concrete planter can make a lovely little corner on any terrace, especially when filled with petunias and forget-me-nots.

Opposite: I love the bright blue pots filled with succulents in the Majorelle garden in Marrakesh, Morocco. Designed in the 1920s, Majorelle was restored by Yves St. Laurent in the 1970s.

final container composition take? What colors work in the container you've chosen and in the setting, as well?

Style

You may swoon over an urn decorated with rams' heads at the garden center, but think twice before you bring it back to your ranch-style house. Observe the architectural detail of your home and the house's setting before you buy, since containers should look at home where you place them.

Contemporary architecture, which at its best is streamlined classicism, calls for the same aesthetics in the containers you choose. Opt for simple, pared down, clean elements of design. And consider strongly architectural plants to complement the containers: acanthus or aloe, perhaps. When a mass of plants appears in a modern setting, I prefer the whole display to be one color.

Simple terra-cotta pots, stone troughs, and wooden tubs look wonderful in rural country gardens, while garlanded pots, carved stone urns, or fancy iron ones lend themselves to more formal situations. These aesthetics are not set in stone (or terra-cotta), however. Sometimes the unexpected can be wonderful.

Form and Scale

Perhaps the biggest mistake we all make with containers is selecting the wrong-sized pot for a particular garden location. Before you buy a container for a spot in your garden, consider how you will view it. Will you see it most often through a window? If you are placing two planted containers on either side of a garage at the end of a

An impressive English lead trough filled with bright petunias makes a strong contrast to the brick wall.

Pale yellow Cape primroses complement the weathered patina of an antique French Anduze pot.

driveway, for example, you want to make sure you can discern color and shape from the entrance of the drive.

In general, I find that larger is usually best. Too many small pots in the landscape get lost and fail to make a statement. I prefer to group my smaller pots on stands or tables and fill them with unusual plants.

To get a sense of the proper scale for a planter you want to purchase, first try a cardboard box of equivalent size in the appropriate spot. Then, once you get a new container home, try it out, much as you would a new lamp or rug indoors, before you fill it. The beauty of garden containers is that most of the time you can return the offending pot for the right one.

The scale and shape of the plants inside the container is important, too. Think about leaf form and size and color. If you're likely to view a container from a distance, choose flowers and leaves with bold shapes and single colors rather than small, wispy arrangements of intermixed flowers, which can be used in closer spaces.

Color

Color is a very personal choice, but in choosing plant material, try to choose colors that work with the container rather than against it.

Pale pink terra-cotta harmonizes with a wider variety of colors than very orange pots. With the latter, it's best to stay with grays, yellow-oranges, and chartreuse, and avoid purples and red. I love the look of soft blues, lavenders, and purples with terra-rossa containers.

Stone containers look beautiful with a combination of

IRON URN   STONE BATHTUB

155

chartreuse-green and deep purple. Also lovely in stone are silver-colored plants like artemisia or helichrysum, with the deep burgundy red or dark mahogany of coleus.

Weathered or green-stained containers are the most natural-looking of the wood containers. I find white Versailles boxes the most challenging to color coordinate, and I usually opt for evergreens or topiary plants instead of flowers. In the dark gray of lead urns, nothing is prettier than yellow with a touch of blue. Try the annual baby blue eyes (*Nemophila menziesii*) with yellow pansies, yellow violas, and white tulips. It helps to take a special pot with you when you visit a nursery to buy plants for it. I discovered through experimentation, for example, that purple pennisetum looks spectacular in my purple-glazed Anduze pot.

REAL GARDENS AND REAL GARDENING

Containers placed thoughtfully constitute a real garden. And the beauty of container gardening is that it is as simple or complex as you choose to make it. A single aloe in an urn, for example, will give you quite a bang for your efforts. If it's the look of an exuberant bouquet you're after, though, container gardening offers the complexity of the perennial border with the added challenge of limited space. And if you're willing to deadhead, cut back, feed, and water container plants as you would those in a border or bed, you will achieve the kind of drama and interest that a pot of impatiens can never provide.

One garden designer recently commented that her biggest challenge is changing the common perception that "you put a spike plant and some impatiens in a pot in the spring, and by gosh, they better last until the first hard frost." It's perfectly okay to fill containers with colorful impatiens. By the end of August, they are wildly overflowing and I think they can look terrific. The drawback is that they are otherwise pretty static, and I believe there's no reason why you can't enjoy in container gardening the same sense of change and surprise that delights you in a perennial border.

You can enjoy change by gardening in three stages throughout the year. Start in spring by filling a stone urn with pansies—perhaps the soft pastel watercolor varieties. When they fade, change to a mixed annual and perennial bouquet for summer, then pop in a pot of perennial grasses in the fall. The planted plastic pots can be put in the cutting or vegetable garden and lifted when needed. When the perennials are finished blooming for the season, they can be transplanted to a woodland or border area before a frost. In winter, fill the stone container with evergreen boughs and red ilex berries. If that sounds too complicated, plant complementary annuals and perennials in a variety of pots, then compose a bouquet with the different pots pulled together in one spot.

Bouquets

To achieve a massive bouquet effect, think of a large pot as you would a small chunk of your border. Cathie Denckla, a Lake Forest, Illinois, designer who creates and maintains exuberant container gardens for her clients, recommends mixing plants with different textures and growing habits—

wispy and light with heavy and bold, spiky and strong with trailing. She combines tall and airy fennel, for example, with cascading ivy, plus larkspur and geraniums. (For some suggested planting schemes, see page 259.)

Cathie also thinks about movement when planting containers. A combination might include fat-leaved succulents, which are tough and unmoving, with lacy-fronded plants that bob in the breeze. Her most memorable—and serendipitous—success with movement came when she placed large pots of tall, graceful grasses near a reflecting pool that featured sculptured swans as fountains. When the wind blew, the whole picture moved.

In planning a bouquet effect in a container, Cathie recommends keeping in mind the relative heights the plants will be at maturity, and the type and quantity of soil required by each. Daisies need a lot of dirt compared to lobelias, for example. Be sure to deadhead, water, and fertilize as you would in a mixed perennial border. Above all, don't be afraid to edit the composition. Pull out unhappy plants and replace them with others.

Standards

Standards are woody plants trained to grow as miniature trees. They have long straight stems and larger, well-formed heads that, in the flowering varieties, can produce a profusion of blooms. Standards offer vertical interest in a grouping of pots. One of these placed near a doorway is lovely; a pair is heaven.

Herbs can be trained as standards or topiary forms. I love growing herbs in individual pots and massing them together, particulary with some trained as standards such as rosemary or bay.

STYLISH STAKING

Stakes in your pots and containers allow you to create a vertical growing surface or to contain an exuberant composition while making a strong style statement. Pyramids can formalize two boxes flanking an entrance, for example, while less formal curly willow or apple branches will control a top-heavy arrangement.

Metal, wood, or twig forms are very appealing in pots. Make sure you use a large pot with plenty of soil and space around the base to accommodate the form. Secure vines and branches with raffia or other natural twine. Even the long foliage of irises works prettily as a tie. But above all, no bright plastic twist-ties!

By tying four bamboo poles at the top with natural twine, you can make a pyramidal frame for vines. Grow 'Heavenly Blue' morning glories in a weathered wooden box near a sunny door. Other wonderful vines include passionflowers, purple bell vine, clematis, and honeysuckle.

CARING FOR YOUR POTS

Almost anything you'd plant in the ground will also work in a container. I've seen lemon trees thriving in Anduze pots for many years. When it's time to move my large pots into the greenhouse for the winter, it is done with a hand dolly, purchased from a large hardware company. Smaller pots used for annuals get emptied, cleaned, and turned over, then wrapped with plastic and covered with burlap.

STANDARD IN VERSAILLES BOX

Chapter Ten: Ornament

Space has an atmosphere,
and what you put into it will color
your thinking and your awareness. . . .
If an object is in the right place,
it's enhanced to grandeur.
More than that, it pleases the inner being
and that, I think, is very important.
That equals harmony.

Louise Nevelson, *Louise Nevelson: Atmospheres and Environments*, 1980[1]

Great design, wonderful plant material, and delightful ornament: A garden becomes a work of art when these three elements are at play. I've seen tiny plots of earth transformed into little Edens by the thoughtful gardener's mastery and combination of these.

This recipe for garden art-making is nothing new. As gardeners throughout the years have sought to perfect their landscapes, to arrange them more to their liking, they have brought culture to nature by introducing objects that heighten the garden experience.

An Englishman, William Lawson, described the formula for garden art-making best when he distilled fifty years of gardening wisdom into his 1618 tome *A New Orchard & Garden*. In a section entitled "Ornament," Lawson spoke to an audience of cottagers whose gardening impetus had been necessity—the growing of food and medicinal herbs for survival. Lawson described the sensual wonder to be had by combining beautiful plants, excellent design, and delightful ornament:

For whereas every other pleasure commonly fills some one of our senses, and that only with delight; {the "new" garden and orchard} makes all our senses swim in pleasure, and that with infinite variety, joyned with no less commodity. . . .

The Rose red, Damask, Velvet, and double double Province-Rose . . . the fair and sweetscenting Woodbine, double and single . . . purple Cowslips. . . . The Violet nothing behind the best, for smelling sweetly. A thousand more will provoke your content.

And all these by the skill of your Gardiner, so comelily and orderly placed in your borders and squares, and so intermingled,

A cast-stone urn placed in a carpet of lily-of-the-valley sets off the lovely shape of this Japanese maple.

that one looking thereon, cannot but wonder to see, what Nature, corrected by Art, can do.

When you behold in divers corners of your Orchard mounts of stone or wood, curiously wrought within and without, or of earth covered with Fruit-trees, Kentish Cherries, Damsons, Plums, &c. with stairs of precious workmanship; and in some corner (or more) a true Dial or Clock, and some Antick works . . . How will you be wrapt with Delight?[22]

In search of Delight in your own backyard, you may find you're eager to experiment with ornament but have some concerns. What's appropriate in your particular garden? "A true Dial," perhaps, or "some Antick"? And where do you put them? What do the old ornamented gardens teach us? I don't think the answers lie in slavishly imitating European or Middle Eastern gardens. But I do think it's worthwhile to look at what, and especially *how,* ornament has been used, then adapt it to our own needs.

Often in our own gardens, we place a statue or some other artifact as an afterthought. We focus instead on getting soil, climate, and plant material to cooperate with each other, as we should. And we put our design energies to work with a palette of growing things, as we should. What we sometimes fail to see, though, is how powerful an ingredient ornament can be when included in that collection of artistic tools.

What constitutes ornament for today's garden? In the following pages you'll find examples of the classics that have served gardeners through the centuries: statues, sundials, and contemporary sculpture, to name a few. But you'll also find ornamental water features, as well as living

art, such as topiary, and attractive functional (and whimsical) items—in short, those accessories, articles, and details that are intrinsically sculptural, and that bring beauty and harmony to your garden.

PLACEMENT

There are any number of practical reasons for including decorative objects in your garden. Ornaments bring your eye up from the ground to help you experience the space better. One ornament can punctuate a small garden or give focus to a large one. Two ornaments placed for classical symmetry will always formalize a setting, while loosely placed ornaments emphasize the casual mood of a garden. In a border, an ornament on a column creates vertical interest; along a woodland path, it creates surprise. The magic of an ornament is not only what it is, but where it's located.

Surprise

It's all in the *placement,* as French gardeners have proven for centuries by creating excitement with statues, urns, and fountains. But I think of an American landscape to illustrate this point. At Wethersfield, the formal Millbrook, New York, garden I described earlier, a wonderful collection of classic statuary is showcased. Near the formal gardens one strolls through a small section of woodland. As you walk through a stand of tall pines and maples, your eye quite unexpectedly is caught by a five-foot bronze statue of Pan, piping away amid the tree trunks. That figure comes as a complete surprise, and in a funny way forces your eye to notice the lovely wild mountain laurel

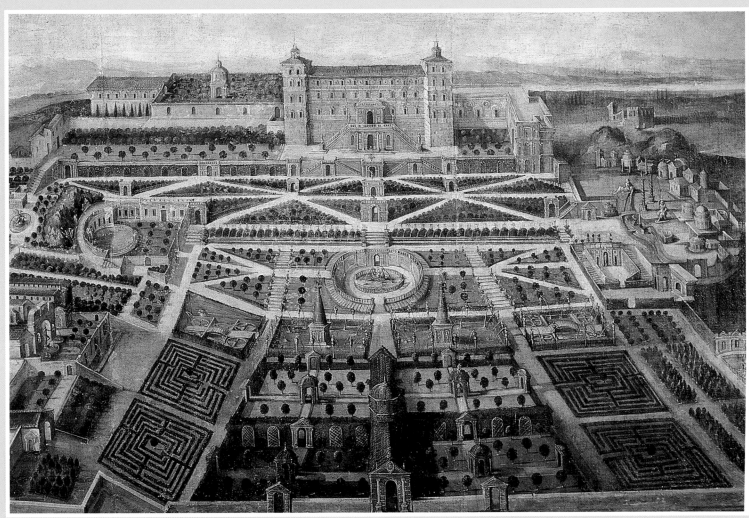

Attributed to Etienne Dupeyac, Gardens of Ippoliti II d'Este at Villa d'Este, Tivoli, *c. 1550-80s. Villa Pietra, Florence.*

Old engravings such as this one of the Villa d'Este are a great source of design ideas for planting patterns.

nearby, the understory of ferns, and the beautiful trees around it. If the figure were not there, you would just keep on walking.

One of the great features of inanimate ornaments is their inherent ability to enhance an animate setting. The very contrast of man-made objects with plant life helps us appreciate the greenery around us. Stone and marble are particularly effective; they are materials from the earth and look natural outside. Juxtaposed with green hedges, grass, and trees, they make the green colors appear even more vivid.

Wood objects, too, enliven green settings. I think of a wonderful spot in the garden of my friend Nancy McCabe that is covered with ferns and hellebores, and beyond that, vast banks of vinca. What makes this spot especially memorable is the weathered wooden chinoiserie dovecote she has used to punctuate the setting and focus the eye. It creates an unforgettable garden vignette.

It also surprises you, as does Pan in the woods at Wethersfield. Using objects in a surprising way can result in a drop-dead dramatic effect. Oscar de la Renta, a passionate gardener, has pulled off such an effect far from New York's fashion runways. At his hilltop home in Connecticut, he enjoys a spectacular 360-degree view of the surrounding hills. A more timid gardener might waffle over how to garden in such a setting. Not Oscar. He has planted an *allée* of pear trees that seems to stretch to the horizon. When you turn the corner and look down this *allée,* you gasp, because he has placed the biggest stone urn you've ever seen on a pedestal, and it's quite literally breathtaking.

An enormous eighteenth-century stone urn is the focal point at the end of the majestic allée of pear trees in Oscar de la Renta's Connecticut garden.

Next page: Jack Lenor Larsen painted his landscape with red azaleas and a corridor of brilliant red posts.

The *allée* controls the vast sky and expanse of nature in a very simple way. It draws you to its end, where you sit and look across a magnificent vista. That's called panache.

Focus and Detail

Ornament gives focus in a vast and overwhelming landscape like the one just described. To bring some kind of magic to a garden that lies next to a spectacular but competing view, you want to make vignettes and focus the eye of the viewer back on the garden in some way. The average gardener doesn't face this dilemma, however. More likely she has to *make* the view, as I do in my own garden. A lot of the ornament I use is there to create interest where there is none. I have a big oil jar, for example, that sits out among the apple trees in the meadow, the view of it framed by an arbor in my formal garden. The jar is white and catches the light in that rustic spot. In spring, one sees the trees blossoming and daffodils blooming under them. Until I placed the jar in their midst, though, no one bothered to look that way. Now visitors are drawn there, and few depart without having explored the meadow.

A very traditional way of employing ornament in the garden is to place it at the center of a garden where paths intersect. In an age-old design that has appeared in millions of gardens throughout history, ornament is used as the central anchor from which the rest of the garden radiates. One of the prettiest and simplest designs to create is a rectangular or square layout with such a central focus. What you place there is up to you, since the ornament you choose is like a piece of jewelry—a very personal statement. You might put an ornate wellhead cover there, or a tall column, or a modern piece of sculpture, as well.

Oscar de la Renta's *allée* illustrates another traditional use of ornament: the placement of a decorative object at the end of two long parallel lines. When an ornament appears at the end of two rows of trees or hedges, your eye is pulled to the farthest point.

You can use salvaged columns from an old building or new ones from a lumber company—ornaments in and of themselves—to make those parallel lines and create perspective. Six columns in a row is an exciting visual focus in a structured garden. If you space the rows far enough apart, you can plant little gardens within the two lines. You may want to paint the columns—even chartreuse is okay in the right context. Or paint them in graduated colors from dark to light so the fading color increases the sense of perspective. Textile designer Jack Lenor Larson has created such an effect in his garden, where wood posts are painted red and gradually fade down in color as they would naturally in a longer view. To enhance the sense of perspective further, you can taper the rows to accentuate the lines rather than place them exactly parallel.

Rows of columns placed in long axial lines is an expression of architecture in nature. It's a technique that was favored in Italian and French Renaissance gardens created by men who were both architects and landscapers— designers who used ornament outside as they did indoors.[3] Long *allées* were lined with rows of statues, almost like artwork lining the hallways of interiors. And at the end of those *allées,* the architect/landscapers placed ornaments as focal points.

Recycled nineteenth-century iron posts linked together with chains enhance this herbaceous border.

While Renaissance designers occasionally erred on the side of too much ornament, I believe contemporary gardeners tend to overlook its potential. To view garden ornaments as baubles, to add them as afterthoughts, is to miss the chance to elevate an outdoor space from merely pleasant to truly artful. Free of any prevailing fashions, modern gardeners can use ornament in formal and informal settings comfortably. The challenge is finding the right piece.

JUST THE RIGHT PIECE

If you've already searched for ornaments, perhaps the following scenario rings a bell. You're standing in the ornament section of the garden center, trying to decide who you are. You thought you knew, until this moment. You came here, after all, to find a focal point for your plantings, not to take a Rorschach test. But the Cupids and rabbits freeze you in your tracks, and the gargoyles seem to ask: "What do you want?"

Selecting a garden ornament shouldn't be so laden with meaning. Yet, when you elevate—quite literally—an object in your garden, the thing you choose takes on importance. Presumably, it's something you will live with for a long time, something that will assert itself in the winter landscape when all plant life has faded.

Ornament is one of the few things in your garden for which you can be held entirely accountable. If a shrub doesn't look right, it could be failing for any number of reasons. If the coneflowers take over while the flax wanes, it's considered the whim of nature, not yours. But an ornament is construed as an expression of your taste.

One's taste alters; but whether it ameliorates or deteriorates is difficult to determine. There can be no absolute in canons of taste; there are only standards, and although these should always be high they should never remain rigid.

Vita Sackville-West, *The Observer*[4]

And when it's painfully wrong, unless it is quite obviously the gift of a well-meaning relative, you're the offender. For that reason, and many others, it's nice to get it right.

While there's an ample supply of bad ornament out there, there's an equal number of wonderful things. And though it's always useful to have an accommodating budget, money is not the main issue here. A scarecrow may be far more stylish in certain gardens than the finest lead urn. This is about choosing something that makes you feel good when you look at it, matching it to the mood of your garden, getting the scale and form right, and placing it thoughtfully.

A MATTER OF TASTE

By the time you're ready to place a piece of sculpture or a fountain, you will have established the garden mood you're after. But personal style develops over time, and you may not be sure what you like. If that's the case, there's nothing like exposure to help define your sensibilities. Look beyond the standard offerings at the garden center to educate your palate: Study magazine photos, scour flea markets, pore over garden books, and visit the best ornament suppliers, if only to see what they offer. You won't know what makes your heart sing until you've explored the choices.

If we conjure up only images of Greek statues as examples of ornament, we are limited by our imaginations. The right ornament for your garden could well be a likeness of Apollo, but it could also be a weathered red wheelbarrow, or a gnarled old jade tree in a pot.

As for my own preferences, I can offer this. I don't much

care for cute ornaments, or ones that are sentimental to the point of sappiness, or those that are just plain unnerving, such as the realistic bronze sculptures depicting the homeowners and their family, usually arrayed in lifelike poses across the lawn. I would, however, delight in four small stone turtles spouting water from each corner of a square pool (but spare me cherubs doing the same). And because I tend to receive the occasional bunny statue, I'm not averse to sticking one in a corner of a bed. As for statues of animals, I'll take a pair of stone dogs, thank you, but not in the likeness of Snoopy.

Setting down hard and fast rules of taste and style only tempts one to break them. While you want to remain consistent with the mood of your outdoor room— choosing a lead trough for an English-style garden, for example—there is an exception for every set-in-stone rule. You might place a very formal statue in a very informal kitchen garden and not only get away with it but make a dazzling statement.

FORM AND SCALE

If American thinking tends toward "bigger is better," we seem to lose our nerve when it comes to decorating our homes and gardens. Inside, we fill our walls with safe little objects and choose relatively small chairs and couches for our rooms. Outside, if we use ornament, it's frequently something safe—say, a small birdbath or statue. There's nothing wrong with small chairs and birdbaths. But some scenarios call for gutsy scale, and when that's the case, it's best not to shrink from it. There's a big sky out there,

and a little tiny cherub lacks the presence needed to stand up to such a backdrop.

In designing an interior, I always deal first with the floor plan, then the walls and the ceiling. I'm continually working to bring the eye up to experience the full height of a room. That's why I like to hang mirrors or pictures up to the ceiling. A sense of height is a critical part of experiencing the full potential of a space, indoors or out.

Before you pick out the perfect sundial or brass crane, it's first necessary to determine the proper scale for an ornamental object. There's no point in buying something two feet tall if you need an object four feet tall. The shape and height and mass you want to express should be your criteria for selection. And you can find unusual things to accomplish your goal, not just the predictable fiberglass statue.

I used this rule of thumb when I went out in search of an ornament to put at the center of my kitchen garden. I wanted something tall and thin, perhaps six or seven feet high. At an antique show, in the middle of a field, I found the answer in the form of a tin lightning rod, set atop a wooden pole, an artifact that in a previous incarnation had served as a weather vane on top of a building. It now decorates my kitchen garden and I don't tire of looking at the patina on the blue tin rod, or the pole's worn red paint, which in fact matches my barn nearby. It does what it's supposed to do—draws the eye upward, toward the sky. A bargain, I think, at a hundred and fifty dollars, and more appropriate than other, more costly choices.

You might wonder how this scale issue relates to your

STONE TURTLE FOUNTAIN

IRON BIRDBATH

STONE BIRDBATH

small garden. Interestingly enough, I find that bold is beautiful in ornaments *especially* in a small garden. Just as large furniture makes a small room more powerful, gutsy scale in garden ornaments has the same dramatic effect. I love the narrow New York city gardens that have walls planted with vines and, at the end of the lot, one very strong ornamental piece. I've just recently done this in a city space where I placed a lattice-covered mirror against the back wall (for an illusion of more garden beyond it), and fronted it with a strong sculpted figure.

Ornaments used in this way are particularly beautiful in winter, covered with snow. These objects hold the garden's structure together when the living bones of the garden—the boldly shaped plants—have disappeared.

Gutsy scale is an acquired confidence for many of us. It is something I have gradually developed and continue to develop. I've also learned to mix large-scale objects with small ones indoors. And since the small objects outside tend to be plants, I've found it makes a dramatic effect to insert a large, strong object in their midst.

The best way to get some height with traditional ornaments, such as sundials or gazing balls or even modern sculpture, is to put them on pedestals. One doesn't think immediately of a pedestal as regulation garden gear, but few items are more useful when it comes to decorating outside.

You can find old pedestals at salvage companies, have them made, buy them new (there's a nice selection out there), or make your own. There are delightful pyramidal lattice pedestals specially made to cradle a gazing ball, or flat-topped, rectangular ones to support an urn or figure.

An old tin lightning rod is placed in the middle of my kitchen garden for architectural interest and to bring height to the center.

STONE DOGS

BRICK PEDESTAL

METAL PEDESTAL

STONE PEDESTAL

With the Hudson River as
a backdrop, a pergola frames
sculpture at the Rockefeller
estate, Kykuit.

White hydrangeas flank
a sculpture by the American
master Augustus Saint-
Gaudens in Jack Lenor
Larsen's garden.

These can be stained white, soft gray or green, or painted blackish green, among other colors. I like to put them in my borders and vegetable garden for vertical effect. But they're also great used in pairs to flank a entrance.

SCULPTURE

One of the most enchanting uses of art in a garden setting occurs in Nelson Rockefeller's sculpture garden in Pocantico, New York. There, important artworks by many sculptors mingle with the green landscape. The piece I recall most vividly is a bronze square sculpted by Henry Moore and mounted on a pedestal. The square frames the trees beyond it and truly enlivens the garden.

The gardens of modern houses often cry out for ornament with a contemporary look. Modern sculptural garden art needn't be restricted to the few families who can afford to buy a Henry Moore. There are fine young sculptors in art schools and communities across the United States who would leap at the chance to create something unique for a garden, something that you can afford. You can find these artists by attending shows sponsored by universities and art cooperatives.

TRADITIONAL STATUARY

Nelson Rockefeller's sculpture garden is a modern version of an old tradition; that is, the use of the garden as an outdoor museum. This tradition seems to have gained popularity during the Renaissance in Italy, a period of great interest in classical thought and design. In a frenzy of antiquity collecting, Roman treasure hunters excavated ruins for ancient Greek and Roman sculpture.

The enthusiasts pulled statues from the ground—many of which were missing arms or legs or noses—to decorate their homes with likenesses of mythical goddesses and warriors. When their houses could hold no more, the statues spilled out into the gardens and became exhibits in these outdoor museums.[6] It was an approach that still appeals to some people today and was one more permutation of the pursuit broadly termed "gardening." In the gardens of antiquity collectors, hedges and trees served as backdrops for the art, subservient to marble and stone.

Besides enjoying the pleasure of showing off their finds, the Renaissance noblemen surely made the discovery every new generation of gardeners makes in time—that stone glows against a backdrop of deep green cypress or yew.

Today the only digging we need to do is through a pile of mail-order catalogs and garden magazines to come up with suppliers of garden statuary. Newly minted statues, in terms of quality and subject matter, range from the ridiculous to the sublime.

Few garden statues are made of carved stone anymore, but there are wonderful, less expensive approximations, just as there are in containers. Artificial stone garden ornaments tend to fall into two categories—clay-based (and fired) or cement-based.

As early as the 1760s, clay-based artificial stone ornaments were being manufactured in England. Perhaps the most famous manufacturer of artificial stone was the Coade family, which dominated the late-eighteenth-century market with exquisite molded vitrified ceramic

A vase should {be} . . . placed upon a firm base . . . either a plinth or a pedestal. . . . {This} gives it a character of art, at once . . . dignified and expressive of stability.

Andrew Jackson Downing, *The Theory and Practice of Landscape Gardening,* 1860[5]

ornaments that often used designs and themes fashionable at the time, including Egyptian sphinxes and lions, pineapples, water nymphs, and river gods. Coade stone ornaments were valued then, as now, not only for their flawlessness, which was owed to the family's secret formula and to the brilliance of the company's mold makers, but also for their ability to weather the elements with few signs of aging. By the time the Coade manufacturing facility went out of business in 1833, it had set a standard by which future generations of fine ornament makers would measure themselves. Today, there are still a small number of ornament makers who pursue the marblelike perfection that the Coade family mastered.[7]

Cement-based ornaments tend to be dry cast or wet cast, depending on the amount of water in the cement formula. Dry cast ornaments, including those called "reconstituted limestone," are generally of a higher quality and price than wet cast. These ornaments, which come very close to the look of real stone, have been packed by hand into usually intricate molds, allowing for details as tiny as eyebrows and fingernails to appear distinctly.

Poured concrete ornaments—the type we see in profusion at garden centers—are generally less detailed but more affordable for the typical gardener. Artificial stone statues often represent classical figures—gods and goddesses, Cupids, children, satyrs, and nymphs.

In choosing an ornament for your garden, I think you have to ask yourself if these classic motifs are appropriate for your garden or if they mean as much to you as they did to the contemporaries of Donatello and Michelangelo.

Greek and Roman mythological figures resonated emotionally with the Italian Renaissance diggers, whose passion for antiquity was fueled by their search for their own classic roots. But more than a replica of the huntress Diana, a piece of an old demolished building may speak volumes to you about your own cultural past.

ARCHITECTURAL ARTIFACTS

In my view, few outings are as much fun as a visit to an architectural salvage company. This is where you'll find, if you're lucky, an urn for your garden that once was a terra-cotta finial on some wonderful, long-departed midwestern building. It may have looked like a small detail at the top of a six-story building, but placed on a pedestal in your garden it will have the presence of a significant artifact.

Other salvaged decorations don't reveal as readily what their new incarnations might be. For example, what do you do with a terra-cotta medallion, two feet in radius, with an acanthus leaf motif? It's beautiful (your name is written all over it), but dare you go home with it? Surely it was magnificent on the side of a theater building at one time, but what the heck do you do with it in your garden?

Consider the possibilities. If it's relatively flat, you could set it into a terrace or path, and it would be wonderful to come upon it in a sea of brick or gravel. Or put it in a place with no traffic—under a glass-topped outdoor table, perhaps, or hanging on a wall adjacent to the terrace. You can also set it into a dry stone wall as a wonderful decorative element. Or simply place it against a tree in a woodland setting so that the stroller finds it unexpectedly.

Other objects can be combined to meet the height and form requirements you have for a particular spot. At Treillage we're continually mixing things up. Four white-painted Greek Revival columns placed on wooden planter boxes, all weathered to approximately the same patina, form a fine colonnade. Another typical *assemblage* recently included a wood pedestal that had once served as the base of a baptismal fount, topped with a nineteenth-century porch column and crowned with a tin pineapple finial. Concocted of elements from different cultures and centuries, it made a wonderfully tall focal point for some garden.

FUNCTIONAL ORNAMENT

Anything you put into your garden has a sculptural quality. If it's visible, it's part of the grand picture. That goes for wheelbarrows, hoses, watering cans, retired Wellington boots, and bins for holding garden equipment. Because our gardens are smaller than those historical estates where garden equipment was hidden in some removed outreach visited only by the minions, everything that shows in our home plots takes on some visual importance. That's why we have to think about where we stack the pots, what the wheelbarrow looks like, and what the best method is for wrapping the hose.

The humblest objects become decorative art in the right hands. I think of my friend Billy Goldsmith in San Francisco, who collects old garden tools and artfully displays them. Little vignettes appear throughout his lovely garden: a row of antique hose nozzles marches across a shelf near his potting table; a collection of sprinkler heads lines

so much depends
upon
a red wheel
barrow
glazed with rain
water
beside the white
chickens
William Carlos Williams,
"Spring and All"[8]

the side of his house. Billy does a lot of potting, especially of succulents. So he has made his pot collection part of the ornament of his garden, and instead of sticking them away, he stacks them up in a charming jumble.

To me, there's no ornament more visually appealing than a gathering of watering cans, carefully collected and thoughtfully placed. It may be a group of disparate shapes and vintages in the collection, or it may be a row of four identical silver galvanized metal cans. Once you've found the right way to display them, they'll have a familiar place in your garden to return to after they're used. And if you're faithful about keeping them organized, like a collection of wooden boxes or antique letter openers on a table, they become decoration rather than clutter when they're arranged nicely.

One of my favorite finds for the store was a beautiful old wooden apple picking ladder, long and tapered. I thought it would look so lovely leaning against a tree in someone's garden, and so did our customers, apparently. I was sorry when the last one went out of the shop.

Sometimes I'm amazed when truly sensitive gardeners, who invest themselves entirely in making beautiful pictures with flowers, shrubs, and trees, introduce distractingly ugly man-made items into those pictures. There are alternatives to bright orange plastic garden equipment if you're willing to search them out. Plastic was never intended to get old. Freshly minted or shabbily worn, there's nothing earthy about a yellow plastic hose holder set against the house. Why not use a forged iron plant hanger instead? As for hoses, who decided that bright green blends into the garden? Give me a black hose any day, one that settles into the dirt like a sunning snake.

I want garden equipment to blend into the scene as much as any item that's designated "ornament." It's fun, too, to find equipment that is intentionally ornamental. The garden faucet can sport a brass frog handle; a set of three teak stake "fenders" with carved pineapple, artichoke, or acorn tops will keep the hose out of the hydrangeas.

Or take a functional item from the past and make it ornamental. Old bell jars, thick glass covers once used to protect plants in cold weather, are wonderful scattered in the kitchen garden. Also delightful are French rhubarb forcers, whether they're forcing rhubarb or not. One woman recently purchased a number of these forcers from the store and made a small wall out of them. Old nongarden items I've found that look charming include a nineteenth-century French iron bathing tub, perfect as a garden trough.

YOUR OWN GRAND TOUR

In the seventeenth, eighteenth, and nineteenth centuries, it was fashionable for English and American aristocrats to make a Grand Tour of European countries. The tour might last for several months, sometimes even years, and when the travelers returned, they often brought back with them art and ornament for their own homes and gardens. Many of these tourists returned from Italy, inspired by its statued gardens, with some original antiquities, but more often they brought back reproductions of antiquities. These objects found homes in formal and cottage-style gardens, as well.

Far left: A weathered teak hose guard stands sentinel, protecting plants from the garden hose.

Left: Birdhouses bring strong vertical form to a garden, as well as lively entertainment when they're occupied.

Opposite: A rusted tin finial sits among the hydrangeas in my shrub border and provides interest long after the blossoms have gone.

A grouping of antique finials with terra-cotta pots covers a beautiful teak table designed by Bill Goldsmith.

Practicality in disguise: A tall gothic finial covers the barbeque, and a weathered wooden cabinet holds tools in Bill Goldsmith's kitchen garden.

When you take your own Grand Tour, whether it's to Mexico or India or Thailand or France, keep your eye out for garden ornaments by observing the pure sculptural and artistic qualities of objects you've never seen before. A copper-lined rice barrel, for example, may present itself as the ideal container for your spades and forks. Or a Thai spirit house, elevated on a column, could make a fantastic central garden focus.

A few years ago I visited India and brought back some wonderful rope beds that I use instead of chaises. These objects have nothing whatever to do with a Connecticut garden, but they work nicely because of their forms. I've found straddle stones in England, which are stone stools that warm in the sun and provide resting spots along the road—not the ideal seating for an American garden, but dandy as rustic ornament.

When you travel abroad, it's wonderful to view the countryside, the gardens, the homes, and the ornaments with an open mind. You don't know when an understanding will hit you, when a pairing of plant colors, perhaps, will spark a concept for the border back home, or when some rather foreign-looking object will suggest itself as a garden ornament. When in doubt, perhaps while you're standing in some faraway bazaar, stick with classical forms to resist being swept away in a moment of bad decision making. On the other hand, spontaneity can create magic.

Pure Form

Obelisks, used in early cultures as primitive sundials, today are sought out for their clean geometrical shapes and their usefulness in adding vertical interest. In the past one found stone obelisks primarily, but there are now many pretty lattice examples available that will support vines beautifully. I love the look of a tall lattice obelisk placed in a border.

Lattice columns have the same effect in the garden: vertical form that brings the eye up and adds another shape into the garden's mix. Certain that my formal garden was missing something, I put four tall lattice columns at each corner of the reflecting pool and, indeed, the whole scheme seemed to come together visually. I did the same with lattice pyramids in the two perennial borders at either side of that pool. Slowly but surely that garden is growing up. What's nice about these sculptural forms is their adaptability. Like the classic Windsor chair, columns, spheres, pyramids, and obelisks are uncomplicated forms that work well in almost any setting.

"True Dials"

An ornament that fits into any garden, the sundial is a classic fixture in gardens. Sundials remind me of earlier gardening times, when a cook might glance over at the dial from weeding chores and hurry off to make supper. For centuries, English gardeners have placed them in the middle of converging paths or in sunny borders.

The sundial we see most often today is the standard model found in gardens throughout the world. It has a metal gnomon that casts a shadow on a platform inscribed with hour lines. Another version is the armillary sphere, a construction of rings used by early astronomers

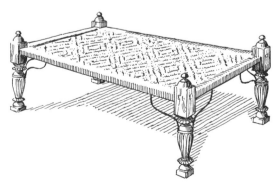

INDIAN BED

WOODEN OBELISK   STONE OBELISK

*What look like giant mushrooms growing in the lawn are
actually straddle stones, which were used in England to elevate
grain houses off the ground to keep pests from the grain.
Giant stone balls are also included in this garden still life.*

to represent the principal spheres of the heavens.

One of the great charms of old-time sundials was the motto, engraved on a plaque fixed to the dial's supporting column. When the motto tradition began is unclear, but its practitioners reveled in chiding the passerby (often in Latin) to hurry on his way, as time was flying. Some were downright morbid, such as *"Sumus fumus"* ("We vanish like smoke"). Not all mottoes were morose, though. One of my favorites from the eighteenth century reads like a toast: "Long may you live/Happy may you be/May the hours move slowly/And from care be free."

Sundials provide focus and vertical form to your garden, and a few well-chosen motto words make the dial an irresistible spot to pause. Sundials, like roses, work best in full sunlight. And if you place it properly, oriented toward the true north, you can use the dial to tell time, as it was intended.

Choose a pedestal of stone or wood that's not so tall that you can't look down on it. At salvage companies you may find pillars or bases of birdbaths, or columns of granite. You can also mount a sundial on a boulder in a more rustic setting.

WATER FEATURES

Water. Cool, soothing water. It was the essence of the earliest gardens, the centerpiece around which pleasure gardens were made. Ancient Persian paradise gardens frequently featured four water channels (symbolic of the main rivers of paradise) emanating from the garden's center and dividing it into four parts, all enclosed within a wall.

Once a function of necessity, wells and fountains in many different cultures were located at the center or close by garden plots in order to make watering easier, and to provide drinking and bathing water.

In our American gardens, water features have played a secondary role at best. But as gardeners discover the many commercially available fountain, trough, and pond possibilities, we are correcting the situation with a frenzy. And while water features aren't necessities today, they bring sound and ornamental shape to the garden and another medium in which to grow plants.

You don't need a Buckingham Fountain to enjoy water in your garden. In fact, the water features that are most memorable to me are those that are simple rather than ostentatious. I think of every little European village I've visited where a charming stone trough caught water from a spigot. I think of a formally hedged and flowered apartment courtyard I sometimes pass in which the sound of a sculptural three-tiered lotus-blossom fountain mesmerizes anyone who stops to rest. Also unforgettable is the graphically simple fountain at Innisfree—a single jet of water that shoots up some twenty feet into the air from a flat base of cut native stones, mimicking the tall narrow tree trunks around it and spraying a mist fit for a Chinese landscape painting throughout the scene. Each of these memorable water features brings an added dimension to the gardens in which they appear: sound, ornamental form, and the *feel* of water.

Water in the garden is attainable for every gardener today at a relatively inexpensive initiation fee. For a minimal cost,

Sundial Mottoes:[9]

Hours fly. Flowers die. New days, new ways pass by. Love stays.

A cunning workman fashioned me, to tell the time of day. Unless a fool should alter me, I'll never go astray.

Horas non numero nisi serenas.

[Latin for "I only count the hours that are serene."]

Old astronomical or navigational instruments such as this armillary sphere become unusual ornaments — and interesting conversation pieces — in the garden.

you can purchase a water-circulating pump that is easily rigged up to a wall or free-standing fountain. Depending on the amount of water you're recirculating, the cost will vary for the basic equipment.

Popular now are small rubber-lined ponds dotting the backyards of many avid gardeners. While I love the planting possibilities, I find only a few pond makers successfully pull off the natural look they pursue. Often the ponds are circled with stone "necklaces" wrapped unnaturally around their perimeters, leaving them looking ill-at-ease in the landscape. The main challenge is to conceal the edge of the rubber pond liner with stones and plantings while making that edge look natural. And because real ponds are quite large, the tiny imitations sometimes look odd to me.

If you want to pursue a naturalistic pond design, I'd strongly recommend studying how ponds look in nature. Examine how rocks are set into a streambed. Study how nature constructs its waterfalls. And when you finally begin building your pond, use native stone and keep it simple.

My own personal preference has been to take a more formal approach. In my own garden, I've built a two-foot-deep rectangular concrete reflecting pool that's clearly man-made; as such it is a sculptural ornament and an extension of architecture into the landscape.

LAURA AND RICK'S POND

When Laura and Rick Talaske purchased their Frank Lloyd Wright prairie-style home in Oak Park, Illinois, in 1990, some of the house had been restored to its 1903 condition, though no traces of the original garden structures—pond, pergola, and wall—remained. With some sleuthing, they found photos taken in 1909 of the garden pond designed by Wright, and they soon undertook to re-create it.

Because part of the original property had been sold off as a lot next door, the couple had to reduce Wright's plan for the pond to one-third its original size. If something was lost in the translation, it's not evident. The genius of Wright is there in the pond's simple but classic shapes and its clever engineering.

Enclosed in a corner of the garden by a stucco wall (also reproduced from old photos) and surrounded by old-fashioned plants, the pond is unified in spirit and style with the house's architecture. The raised concrete surround of each section makes a graphic rectilinear pattern on the ground.

At first glance, the pond appears to be three ponds—one long rectangular one and two smaller square ones opposite it. But in fact, the eleven-by-eleven-foot square, two-foot-deep concrete pond is bridged by a sidewalk that runs across its middle. Another concrete sidewalk/bridge meets the first at a right angle, making a T, and cutting the second rectangle into two smaller squares.

The pond is bursting with life in summer—frogs and comets ("Dimestore goldfish," says Laura, "three-fifty a dozen"), plus an assortment of plants. The different geometrical sections act as separate containers for the plantings Laura has selected for each. In the long rectangle, she has planted bog specimens—yellow flag iris (*Iris Pseudacorus*), giant arrowhead (*Sagittaria latifolia*), dwarf

papyrus (*Cyperus haspans*), pickerel rush (*Pontederia cordata*), and mosaic plants that spread like stars across the surface of the water.

One of the small square ponds fairly explodes with the green waxy leaves and lavender blossoms of water hyacinths. The other square pond holds water lilies, and sometimes the sailboats of their small son, who can perch quite comfortably on the concrete wall that rises a foot above ground level.

The goldfish swim around in the tank below and make appearances in all three pond openings. It's a bit of whimsy that Wright undoubtedly built in for the enjoyment of the children as well as the adult owners. The pond itself seems like a message from the past, almost a gift, from the master.

Granted, the Talaskes' pond is remarkable in its design, but the material in it is common stuff: concrete, reinforced by heavy metal rods and poured in place. Unless you're highly skilled with concrete, though, enlist the help a landscape designer or experienced contractor for a pond of any complexity. He can also introduce you to the many wonderful molds available for concrete pool coping, the decorative edge that surrounds a formal pond.

Of all the charms that recommend water in your garden, more than any other aspect, sound is primary. For a small investment of time and money, you can mask traffic noise, soothe your soul, and trickle and splash atmosphere into your garden with water.

TOPIARY: "ANTICK WORKS" AND OTHER PLEASURES
Why outdoor topiary—the shaping of trees and shrubs

So far and still it is that, listening,
I hear the flowers talking in the dawn;
And where a sunken basin cuts the lawn,
Cinctured with iris, pale and glistening,
The sudden swish
Of a waking fish.

Amy Lowell, from "Behind a Wall"[10]

The pond at this Frank Lloyd Wright house in Oak Park, Illinois, echoes the simple, classic lines of the house.

*Man is a maker
of patterns: to impose
symmetrical or
significant shape on
things, even on living
creatures, is one of
his deeper pleasures.*

Edward Hyams,
English Cottage Gardens,
1970[11]

into forms—is making a comeback in recent years is a bit of a mystery, since our typically small American gardens hardly resemble the formal estates of the 1920s, where great obelisks and spheres and chess pieces (maintained by an army of gardeners) might appear right at home on the vast residential grounds. I suspect the current enthusiasm has much to do with recent excitement about gardening in general. As Americans become more sophisticated gardeners, we see topiary as one more facet of the art to explore. You may find yourself thumbing through a gardening magazine one day, come upon some topiary figure, and say, "I want to try that."

That's precisely what happened when I undertook to give a topiary bird, sphere, and cylinder a home in my own garden. A friend led me to the ramshackle greenhouse of an elderly topiary grower who was selling off his remaining stock about fifteen years ago. I brought three sad-looking shrubs home with me, all roughly columnar in shape and sporting a form of indeterminate identity at the top of each, and all the worse for wear from neglect. With much love and trimming, the yews began to resemble what the old man had envisioned, and I was soon hooked on pruning. Today they are about twelve feet tall and line the edge of a sidewalk near the house, making a whimsical hallway of the space.

For centuries the art of topiary was favored by formal gardeners who celebrated their mastery over nature by clipping yew trees and boxwood into fanciful shapes. In practicing this green art, the gardener becomes sculptor, and the tree or shrub becomes the artist's medium.

Topiary's practitioners date back to the first century in Rome, where the subject of the garden sculptor might have been a sailing ship or the initials of a villa's owner.[12] In fact, the highly valued Roman who carved the ornamental green forms was called a topiarius. In time, topiary figures found their way into gardens in the Netherlands, Germany, France, and England. Adopted by the aristocracy, topiary art decorated eighteenth- and nineteenth-century English gardens and occasionally depicted such ambitious themes as fox hunts. Topiary also spread into cottage gardens; when the gardeners at the great estates went home, they brought with them the expertise to sculpt peacocks in their own privet. The European fancy for topiary soon took root in American soil, along with boxwood edging, in the formal gardens of wealthy immigrants in the middle and southern colonies.

At Versailles, the seductive charm of topiary even adapted itself to the art of seduction. In *Madame de Pompadour,* author Nancy Mitford describes a 1745 masked ball at which King Louis XV, attired as a yew tree clipped in the shape of a column with an urn on top, swept the lovely Madame de Pompadour off her feet. The smitten beauty promptly left her husband and embarked on a twenty-year love affair with the king.[13]

You may not be ready to leave your husband for a clipped yew tree, but you may be ready to clip a yew. A fair warning is in order, though. As Madame de Pompadour discovered, pursuing topiary is not for the faint of heart. It is rather an *affaire de cœur,* and requires a long-term commitment.

There's nothing in gardening that better shows off what you can do than to create and maintain a beautifully pruned form, whether it's one shrub, a hedge, or a tree. Topiary gardens in the past, though, were created by people who had wealth and plenty of gardeners, while today's gardener is likely to be doing the work herself. That's why it makes sense to begin modestly, perhaps with one or two forms.

Choose as mature a specimen as you can afford, and make sure its roots become well-established, since you'll be clipping away on it perhaps twice a year. Your chosen shrub will need plenty of sunlight, on all sides if possible. The Japanese yew is an excellent variety to choose, but there are many other options, including hollies, boxwood, hemlocks, arborvitae, and spruces. For the novice topiarist, a wonderful resource for patterns, history, and advice is *The Complete Book of Topiary,* by Barbara Gallup and Deborah Reich.[14]

You can choose a shrub that approximates the design you want to achieve or use a topiary form to make a perfect shape. I prefer the latter, since it's extremely difficult to see what you're doing when you're balanced on a ladder looking down. These forms are available through mail order or at select garden shops. (See Resources.)

For the gardener who wants a large, strong form as ornament, the topiary shrub works in place of more expensive conventional sculpture. And while topiary shapes are usually associated with formal gardens, I think they can work well in other contexts, too. Line them up, or match them in pairs for a formal look. Or use a topiary chicken, or spiral, or obelisk as a delightful focal point at the center of an informal kitchen garden. As with other garden ornaments, it's all in the *placement.*

CLIPPED BAY IN POT   YEW SQUARE WITH BALL   TIERED TOPIARY FORM

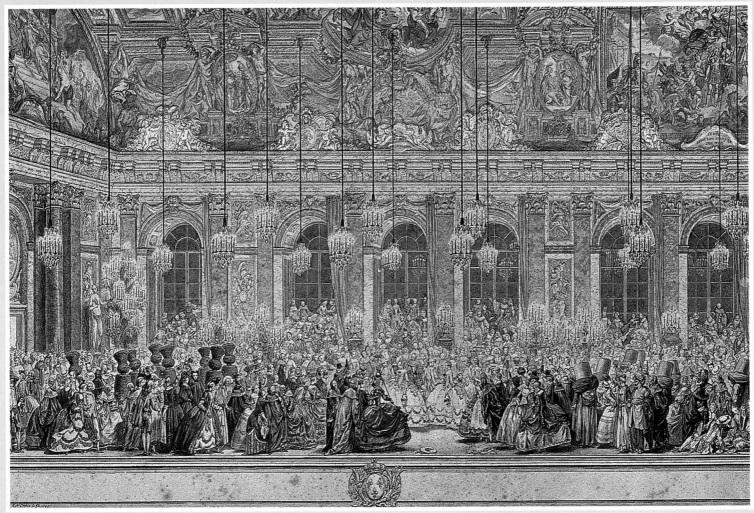

Charles-Nicolas Cochin, The Ball of the Clipped Yew Trees in the Galerie des Glaces, February 25, 1745. *Louvre, Paris.*

Louis XV and his courtiers understood the importance of garden ornament when they went dressed as yew trees to a ball in 1745.

Chapter Eleven: Furniture

Lazy mornings under the trees with a fat new novel, iced tea in the afternoon, sweet corn roasted over an evening fire, with children and friends gathered around. Summertime insists that we live out-of-doors and we happily oblige, moving meals, social gatherings, and quiet time out into the open air. Our gardens become our living and dining rooms, and for those few months, at least, we revel in the sounds and smells of the earth as we go about our lives.

Having worked hard to create wonderful rooms in nature—from the terrace to the private woodland spot— even the most possessed gardener wants a place to call it quits for the day, to sit back and savor his or her good efforts. It's a just reward, after hours on your hands and knees, to have a favorite seat waiting for you.

Furniture enhances the roomlike quality of an outdoor space, just as it transforms empty rooms indoors. It makes a space more welcoming. And it communicates to visitors (quite literally when a seat is placed near flowers in bloom): Stop and smell the roses.

What that seat looks like depends on the gardener's priorities and tastes and its location in the garden. In choosing furniture, particularly brightly colored pieces, ask yourself: Do I want to look at this bench more than I want to look at the garden? In short, you need to decide whether a particular piece of furniture will be a prominent feature or will nearly disappear, whether it will distract from the garden or create a wonderful vignette.

In my own garden, the trees and plants are the main attractions and I prefer garden furniture to play a quiet

Brightly painted Arts and Crafts chairs suggest a friendly conversation.

secondary role. A dazzling sofa or chair might be the *pièce de résistance* that gives focus to a living room I design, but that's not the effect I'm after outside. I prefer my peonies, rather than the chaise, to steal the show. Nonetheless, I have seen brightly painted benches and chairs used to wonderful effect in natural settings. To better understand what's appropriate in your own garden rooms, it's helpful to look at the terrace separately from the rest of the garden.

LIFE ON THE TERRACE

The terrace earns its keep in balmy weather. It's the scene for our most intense outdoor living—cooking, sunning, eating, socializing, and viewing the garden. That's why comfortable seating is a must, for both guests and bone-tired gardeners.

If you have the luxury of planning a terrace before it is built, consider which activities will occur there and what furniture you'll need before you define its dimensions in stone. But if you already have a terrace, acquaint yourself with the space requirements of garden tables and chairs before you buy. In both cases, a clear traffic path from house to garden is essential, as well as adequate room to move chairs in and out from a dining table. Scale counts, too. You want the furniture to relate in size to the terrace rather than overcrowd it.

Because terrace furniture is close to the house, it looks best when it ties into the style of your home. It should complement your house's exterior and the rest of the garden the way sofas and chairs complement your living room. This really isn't much of a leap to make, since we tend to buy houses in the taste we like. The right garden furniture will enhance the house by responding to it. Contemporary garden furniture, for example, will make a contemporary garden all the more powerful a design statement.

How you group the furniture will affect how you use the space. In decorating living rooms for clients, I always try to group chairs in such a way as to allow conversation: a sofa with a pair of chairs pulled up next to it, for example, or a gathering of several chairs around a low table. Even when they're not all in use, such gatherings of objects make a friendlier statement than one lone chair.

Practical Issues
Living in New England, I have learned a few lessons about the value of durability in garden furniture. One year, smitten by a wonderful twig chair, I placed it in my garden, only to find it in shreds by September. Furniture has to be sturdy to survive New England's temperamental climate and I have since come to pay the weather its due respect.

When you choose furniture for your terrace, you should consider some very practical issues: how it will weather and where and how it will be moved if it can't stay outside. Is there a place to store all that rattan stuff? Do you really want to haul in a wrought-iron dining set every fall? In a warm climate where furniture is outside permanently, it makes sense to choose something a bit more solid than a wicker chair. If you live in a cold climate, on the other hand, portability may drive your decisions. A set of folding chaises will take up far less of the basement than a set of wrought-iron chairs.

The weather is always doing something there; always attending strictly to business; always getting up new designs and trying them on people to see how they will go. But it gets through more business in spring than in any other season. In the spring I have counted one hundred and thirty-six different kinds of weather inside of twenty-four hours.
Mark Twain on New England weather[1]

Garden furniture is available in many materials today, and each type has its own qualities to recommend it. Wood is terrifically adaptable to any number of settings and it weathers well. Aluminum is highly portable. Stone can stay out all year and contributes a sense of permanence to a setting. Wrought and cast iron offer rich and historical texture to the garden. The type you choose will have everything to do with your climate and space restrictions.

Eclectic or Suite—Finding the Balance

Gladly, times have changed since the days when newlyweds bought suites of furniture—whole sets of matching pieces—for living or dining room or bedrooms. It's much more fun to mix and match. I love the texture and personality that result from a meeting of styles and periods. That's why it's a bit disconcerting when one sets out to purchase garden furniture and discovers the suite concept alive and well in outdoor furniture showrooms. Confronted with the possibilities, one wonders: Should I get the six chairs, the matching table, the matching sofa, the side chairs, *and* the matching chaise?

I find complete suites of garden furniture—whether it's wrought iron or teak—to be heavy-looking and overdone. On the other hand, too many disparate pieces mixed together look cluttered and distract from the garden. What's the happy balance?

I think terrace furnishing calls for some controlled mixing. Dining accommodations, for example, look great when four or six matching chairs are paired with a table of different materials. Wrought-iron or metal folding chairs with a slatted wood or stone table fit the bill, or wooden chairs around a metal-based table. For relaxing and conversing beyond the dining area, a sofa and a complementary pair of chairs are perfect.

Color

As important as form and style is color. A gathering of brightly colored furniture is something like a group of rowdy guests on a terrace: What you notice first is the noise and then, all those legs! The crowd may be there to experience the garden, but ultimately they just distract from it.

An orange braided plastic folding chair near a verdant garden is an unwelcome intrusion. Garish, it is the object the eye catches first, rather than the lovely shape of a tree. For that reason, and because there's typically a lot of it, I prefer to keep terrace furniture in a neutral tone. Black and dark green are common manufacturer's colors, for good reason: They harmonize, rather than compete, with grass and shrubs. Even traditional white furniture can sometimes draw too much attention to itself. (Look at black and white photos in old garden books to comprehend this effect—the white pops out at you.)

It's important to tie in the color of the garden furniture to the palette used in the house's exterior, since the house is usually the backdrop. If your home is stone, dark green or gray furniture is better than white. But if it is white clapboard or weathered shingles with white trim, then white furniture will look just fine. With dark green trim, for example, consider dark green furniture.

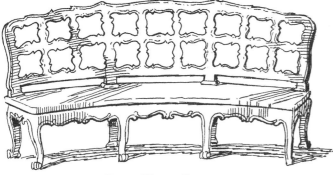

CURVED WOODEN BENCH

WOODEN BENCH FROM DUMBARTON OAKS

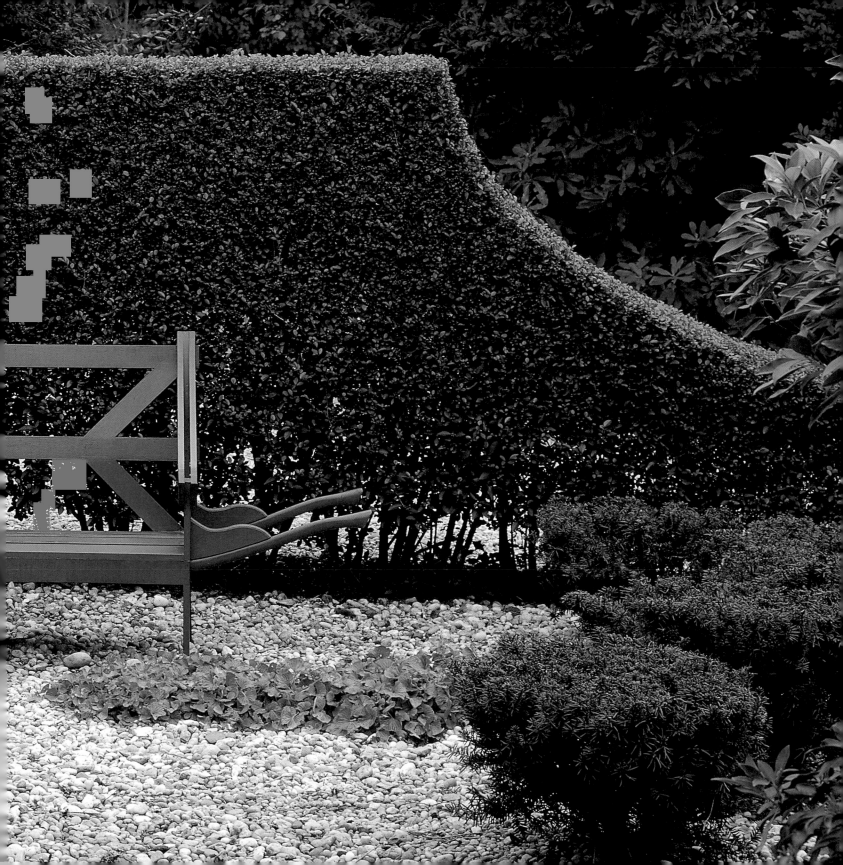

A row of green wooden rockers line up on this lawn without distracting the eye from the landscape.

Modern chaises harmonize with a modern pool in a setting on Maryland's Eastern Shore.

Pages 192-193: A sculptural barrow bench echoes the form of a Long Island garden hedge.

Furniture cushions call for the same restraint. A neutral solid color or stripe blends in. A riotous and ruffled print does not.

What to do with all those interesting, mismatched garden chairs you've picked up at flea markets? Paint them all the same neutral color. It will unify the assemblage, making the pieces less confusing to look at as a group.

OUT IN THE GARDEN

When it comes to furnishing private spots out in the garden, you may toss out any or all of the previous guidelines. One seat is dandy if you prefer to sit alone in the woods listening to birds. And the style of the seat, away from the house, can be entirely different in mood. Comfort is nice, but not essential. A wrought-iron bench that requires one to sit upright might not be your choice for the terrace but it could be perfect as a stopping point in the woods. Neutral colors? Certainly appropriate, particularly if you want to come upon the seat unexpectedly, but not the only option. A well-designed, colorful bench will work as an accent piece and be perfectly tasteful because it is one strong object rather than four or five. Practicality? Upholster a bench in moss if you want to. And don't worry if a painted surface is flaking or rusty if you like the way it looks. Some garden seats are purely ornamental. If you do plan to sit out in the garden, place the seat for maximum comfort and garden viewing—in shade or sun, depending on what you want.

It seems odd to me that, for all the work we do in the garden, we don't take much time to sit out there beyond the terrace. If that rings true for you, it's easy to fix. Put a table in the woods. Pull a chair up to the roses. Mow a path to a drooping tree and park a chair under it. Place a bench by the pond so you and your young friends can watch the frogs. Make a room where there was none before, then go *sit* in it.

ACCESSORIES

What makes a space a room, anyway? Besides the enclosing walls, certainly it's a piece of furniture that provides a focal point and a place to sit. But it's also the objects we hang on the walls and the favorite things we add to the furniture to personalize and pull together the whole picture.

Outside, as in, it's fun to arrange a collection of favorite things in one spot. Put together a group of objects you love—perhaps old wooden finials, or stone architectural fragments, or hand-blown mercury glass gazing balls, or weathered birdhouses, or small wire baskets and topiary forms—and arrange them on an old table next to the house. Or hang a group of terra-cotta masks on a garden wall. At my own home, I have gathered together some of my favorite small pots atop a table. They get far more attention there than they would scattered throughout the garden.

On a loggia, consider adding a mirror to make the space seem larger and to reflect the light and greenery of the garden. And be sure to place pots and urns on your terrace along with the furniture, as well. A grouping of pots helps one avoid the peculiar feeling that you're part of a teak or wrought-iron furniture ad. Try one or two large oil jars,

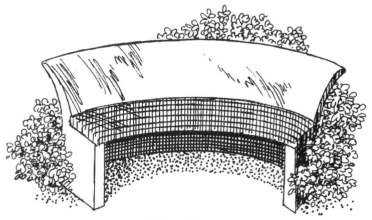

MODERN BENCH

depending on your terrace's size, or an arrangement of several smaller ones.

THE CLASSICS

Garden seats have come a long way since turf, fresh cut from the meadow and placed atop dirt mounds, was the favored sitting (or leaning) spot in medieval European pleasure gardens. Today, while we can pick and choose from a plethora of traditional and modern garden seats, several models have remained favorites over the long haul. Following are a few of the greats.

The Stone Bench

In A.D. 62, Pliny the Younger, a wealthy Roman who owned two country places besides his town house, described in a letter to his friend Appolinaire his pleasure garden Tusci, in the Apennine foothills, which included "a semicircular bench of white marble, shaded with a vine which is trained upon four small pillars of Carystian marble."[2]

Marble and carved stone benches in the Italian style, whether curving or straight-lined, have been part of classic gardens for centuries. Today, the models one finds in this tradition are likely to have been made of concrete and sprung from a mold. Still, the classic design motifs that Pliny would have admired, such as the acanthus leaf, appear in many reproductions and are redolent of Italian gardens.

Stone benches are not intended for long sitting spells, though Pliny apparently dined at length on his. Rather they are picturesque sculptural forms, often used at the end of a long path or *allée*, or set amid flowers and greenery.

Nearly immovable, they hold their own in the profusion of summer and give you something wonderful to look at when snow claims the garden.

The Chippendale Bench and Chair

When trade opened up with China in the eighteenth century, England was swept away with a passion for chinoiserie, objects ranging from porcelain to furniture that were inspired by imagined and real Chinese design. William Halfpenny's 1750 pattern book *New Designs for Chinese Temples, Triumphal Arches, Garden Seats, Palings, etc.,* was the first pattern book to introduce an eager public to garden furniture "in the Chinese taste." Chair and bench designs were angular geometrical pieces with lattice-patterned backs and straight legs. Thomas Chippendale elaborated upon the style in his 1754 pattern book for household furniture, *Gentleman and Cabinet-Maker's Director.*[3]

What fascinates me is that Chinese design motifs were present from the very beginning of pleasure gardening in this country. There were fretwork fences in Colonial Williamsburg gardens, evidence that chinoiserie had admirers in the New World.

Though chinoiserie's popularity has waxed and waned over the centuries, the influence of the "Chinese Chippendale" style in garden furnishings persists. Of all the classic garden seat designs, the Chippendale-style wood chair and bench are most at home in nearly any setting. I find their clean lines attractive not only in traditional settings but in very modern ones, too, despite the fact that they originated over two hundred years ago.

SOD BENCH

Nature provided the moss cushion on this English stone bench in my garden.

A *living* bench is created by stone slabs with cascading succulents growing wild through the stone wall that forms the back.

The Fern Bench

When the Industrial Revolution presented new garden seat possibilities in the form of cast iron, Victorians leaped at the chance to add these catalog offerings to their gardens. Cast-iron technology allowed for far more intricate patterns than wrought iron, and many of the new cast benches featured designs based on forms from nature: grapevines, morning glories, passionflowers, blackberries, and, particularly from 1870 to 1890, ferns.[4]

Today the fern bench is made in cast aluminum from those early designs. Antique originals are still around and I've had the good luck to have a few in my stores. The most beautiful one I ever had at Treillage had rusted to a glorious shade of brown—exactly the color of ferns as they fade in autumn. Had I kept it for myself, I would have placed it in the midst of living ferns, just as it was. When a customer bought the bench, she asked that we paint it. While it wasn't an unusual request. I found that I simply couldn't bring myself to do it, and I wished her well in having it painted on her own.

Such judgment calls are strictly personal, but for me, the choice was clear—patina over practicality. A cast-iron bench, newly painted, will never provide truly comfortable seating. So why not use it as it functions best—as a decorative piece, aged to the color of a fall woodland?

Rustic Furniture

Rustic garden furniture is made from the trunks, branches, and roots of trees, usually unstripped of their bark. The primitive look was a natural fit for the Romantic landscape parks that wealthy English landowners favored in the eighteenth century.

In the United States, rustic garden style was embraced by America's first important landscape designer, Andrew Jackson Downing (1815–1852). Downing, who adapted the English landscape style to American settings, preferred rustic garden structures as appropriate furnishings for the picturesque style he devised for rural cottage residences. And at the turn of the century, American tycoons chose to decorate their "great camps" in the Adirondacks with chairs, tables, benches, and garden shelters created from the trunks of native trees.

Today, rustic furniture is enjoying yet another revival as American craftspeople fashion furniture, pavilions, arbors, gates, fences, even bridges with the trunks and branches of poplar, hickory, laurel, willow, and eastern red cedar trees. These rustic garden furnishings look especially appealing set out in the woods or in a meadow, where they blend with the natural setting.

The Lutyens Bench and Chair

You've seen it before in garden magazines. It's the Lutyens bench, designed by Gertrude Jekyll's collaborator, the architect Sir Edwin Lutyens. Lutyens seems to have adapted the English wooden park bench by giving it slats and a prettier shape. The teak Lutyens chair and bench are wonderful garden furnishings, but happen to be suffering from overexposure at the moment. If you purchase either a bench or chair in this style, it's nice to mix it with other things.

FERN CHAIR   FROND BENCH

Top left: Willow chairs and a gnarled tree trunk make a rustic vignette in this inviting courtyard.

Above left: Teak steamer chairs are comfortable seating, the weathered gray color harmonizing with the stones and house.

Top right: Cast-stone table and chairs simulating tree trunks create an interesting setting.

Above right: I combined a cast-stone table with an assortment of French metal chairs on my own kitchen terrace as a place to have coffee in the morning sun.

Adirondack Chair

Ironically, the Adirondack chair did not originate in the Adirondacks and it does not resemble, in its clean angular lines, the irregular and natural form of rustic furnishings associated with that part of the country in the early twentieth century. Patented in 1905 as the Westport chair, the design later came to be called the Adirondack chair.[5]

The Adirondack chair's design is classically American: rugged, practical, and simple yet elegant. It is roomy and perfectly comfortable without cushions, and sports arms wide enough to accommodate drinks, and feet substantial enough that they won't sink into the grass. Out on the lawn, it looks appropriate in a traditional or more contemporary setting.

You can leave the Adirondack chair to weather to a subtle gray, or paint it any color you can think of. Several look terrific lined up in a row, or gathered in a circle.

The Steamer Chair

For most of us the idea of transoceanic travel conjures up visions of squashed elbows in the doubtful luxury of a 767. Ah, for the days of the civilized chaise, when intercontinental travel meant a week or so of enforced quiet with no engagement more pressing than watching the waves pass by.

Placed on the lawn or poolside, the steamer chair suggests the delicious repose of the *Queen Mary.* On the terrace or lawn or near a swimming pool, it's nice to line up two or more identical chaises for a neat graphic look. I have four of them on the lawn overlooking the formal lower garden.

Modern Furniture

For contemporary houses and gardens, simple metal or wood outdoor furniture can be suitable. There is wonderful metal and nylon-mesh furniture that enhances any modern terrace; wood furniture made along very simple, angular lines can also look marvelous.

THE POTTING TABLE

Potting tables are necessities for gardeners who do a lot of container planting. My friend Billy Goldsmith is one of those people, and he worked out a very clever design. The table is a rectangular teak one, with a slatted top that allows him to brush dirt off when he's finished. Beneath the table are two bins (garbage cans would do, if you decide to make your own table). These contain potting soil that is already mixed. Also beneath the table are shelves to one side that are there for pots and tools. The potting table can be a decorative feature, as well, on which a charming arrangement of empty and planted pots can reside.

Tables not intended as potting surfaces can be used for that purpose nonetheless. I once sold a wonderful old French candy-making table, which had wrought-iron ends, a zinc top, and a serrated or notched tin edge around it. It was headed for someone's garden and couldn't have been a more perfect potting surface.

GARDEN FURNITURE ON A BUDGET

One of my favorite things to do is rescue old furniture, garden or otherwise. If you're willing to put in a little time at tag or estate sales, you may come away with nice pieces

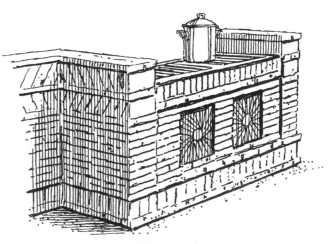

MOROCCAN GRILL

at very reasonable prices. At auction houses, for example, interior furnishings make it to the gallery but garden furniture often doesn't even get cataloged, and a whole set of it may go to a buyer who's willing to take it away for around a hundred dollars.

I still find that you can get good older furniture for a lot less money than you can buy the new high-end, well-designed garden things. Older wrought-iron furniture is heavier, in fact, than what is made today.

Check old pieces carefully before buying. Rusted iron furniture may not be stable, for example. If the piece passes inspection, cover it with a clear coat of rustproof spray to prevent further deterioration. Every few years, repeat this procedure to protect the piece. Old furniture can also be stripped and repainted if you prefer a more perfect finish or wish to change the color.

OPEN-AIR COOKING

Few pleasures are more satisfying than cooking outside, but the aesthetic appeal of barbecue grills leaves something to be desired. Even if you own a top-of-the-line gas grill, I think it's best to find a place to conceal it.

If you do a lot of outdoor grilling, try to anticipate how you will cook before you construct a terrace. You can build in your own cooking pit with bricks, for example, and a grill top, or make a bay attached to the house as a hideaway for an existing grill. Or fit a grill into an outside fireplace. In any case, be sure your cooking apparatus is out of sight from the spot where you dine. I have seen many a lovely terrace, set for dinner, ruined by an unattractive grill.

IV

PLANTING WITH STYLE

Chapter Twelve: Inspired Planting

California hillside gardening doesn't much resemble the kind of gardening I do on my flat, viewless piece of Connecticut land. My task has been to create my own views and to develop vertical interest wherever I can. Not so for many West Coast gardeners, who often have vistas to die for. But when it comes to the garden, chances are the land for the garden plot is headed downhill at a hair-raising angle. Such a scenario presented itself to my friend Nancy Goslee Power, transplanted Connecticut native, garden designer, and author of *The Gardens of California.* Her client, architect Dick Martin, had built a wonderful modern stucco and glass house atop a Los Angeles–area hill and took a great personal interest in developing the garden along with Nancy. They knew it had to be bold to stand up to the house's strong architecture and color (a coral-raspberry shade Nancy calls Roman red), but what to do with that hillside?

The obvious choice, one pursued by many hillside gardeners, was to terrace. But, inspired by the property's undulations, Nancy and Dick planned a garden that from a distance resembles an abstract painting. Great brush strokes of color dash across the hill, punctuated by columnar Italian cypresses and the blue-gray spikes of *Agave Americana.* It's all planted into the angled hillside and is crisscrossed by an earth-colored decomposed granite path.

Walking the path, a visitor is pulled through a stunning natural diorama in which plant forms assert themselves against bold sweeps of color. A river of chartreuse grasses runs between the purple bank of lavender above it and a strip of deep green-leaved pink proteas (*P. neriifolia* 'Pink Ice')

The hillside of this California garden is transformed with the tapestry of textures created by contrasting leaf forms.

below it. Around a bend in the path, the "Mediterranean border" appears. Great five-foot mounds of *Echium fastuosum* 'Pride of Madeira,' the bluish purple spires of which have earned its title as the "delphinium of the south of France," serve as a backdrop, along with the fat pincushionlike chartreuse spires of *Euphorbia Characias* 'Wolfenii'. In front of these masses, silver-leaved Mexican sage and red fountain grass complete a dramatic tableau.

Many combinations are simple—two or three plants—yet dramatic. A group of small eucalyptus trees (*Eucalyptus torquata*) are combined with the fleshy, silver-blue leaves of the coral-blooming *Aloe striata*. Near the house's entry, fat-leaved, eggplant-black *Aeonium arboreum* 'Zwartkop' serves as an underplanting for a grouping of purple hop bush (*Dodonaea viscosa* 'Purpurea').

Descending the path takes time, since you are inclined to stop frequently to study the views ahead, then turn around for yet one more extraordinary picture. At the bottom of the hill on level ground is a placid resting spot called the "Moon Garden." Here you sit in solitude on a twig chair amid a stand of blue gum trees and a soft carpet of buffalo grass. The spectacular views to be glimpsed at various points from the hillside are entirely obscured in the Moon Garden by the enclosing black acacias.

I mention the garden because it embodies what great planting style means to me. There are open spaces and private rooms. It is constantly surprising at every turn. And Nancy and Dick have used form, scale, texture, and color fearlessly. As a result, the Martin garden is a work of art.

CHOOSING PLANTS

There are so many wonderful books and magazines chock-full of plant combinations and exciting ideas that I rarely feel at a loss for inspiration in my own garden. Equally exciting are the catalogs that arrive in late winter when I am most vulnerable, when some new offering is likely to leave my heart pounding. Inevitably I succumb to at least a couple of finds. This impulse buying is contrary to my best reasoning, but I've found a way to accommodate both head and heart on the subject. When I can't resist some spectacular new plant but haven't a clue where I'll place it, I know that the kitchen garden can take in one more stray until it finds a permanent home.

Having a framework allows me that latitude. In my first, structureless garden, I relied on perennials to *be* the garden. Now I can buy a few perennials and if they work, that's great. But if they don't, the garden doesn't go away.

Aside from the impulse buys, though, are the structural mainstays of the garden, and the thematic choices that contribute substance and mood. What plant would be fabulous next to the Russian sage in the perennial border? What would most beautifully cover the lattice obelisks? For those decisions, I think first about where the plant will be located and from what point it will be viewed. Over time, I have learned to value foliage, to think big, to seek out texture and interesting form, and to plant what thrives.

Choose for Foliage

There was a time in my evolution as a gardener when the flower a plant produced was the reason I chose it. But

Most of Tuscany today is cultivated and clipped; the spring countryside is laid out in delicate swatches of green: yellow-green of young corn and wheat, blue-green of rye, across which march, as if in spring maneuvers, files of silver-green olive trees, yellow-green figs, blue-green

copper-sulphate sprayed grapevines, wheeling, fanning in and out, deploying, while the blackish-green cypresses and parasol pines, always seen in profile, silhouetted along a hilltop or on a slope, stand at attention, a windbreak, against the pale-blue sky.

Mary McCarthy, *The Stones of Florence*[1]

flowers are often fickle, arriving for only a short time or not at all. So I've learned to appreciate the steady pleasures of a plant's foliage. I've come to see the leaf as equal to the flower.

When I need a plant for the perennial border, I think first in terms of its potential scale, its texture, and, of course, its form and color. How will its shape and scale work with other elements in the spot I have in mind? Will it grow large enough to be viewed from my screened porch? Will it work best in a mass? How does its texture "read" from a distance? Does its color offer something I need?

Choose for Scale
I've talked about scale throughout this book, but I think it bears repetition in relation to choosing plants. Don't shy away from *big*. If you have a garden where everything is low and tiny, you'll never achieve any sort of excitement.

Large scale helps you feel the space. Strong vertical elements draw your eye up, allowing you to experience the height of the garden. If you are planning a garden for a new house set in a cow pasture—a blank slate with no existing trees—remember to plant tall trees that will be coming along with your lower trees and hedges.

Begin with Anchors
You must begin with strong massive elements to hold the garden together; once they're in place, you can then add lots of little plants if you wish. Big things are your anchors. Whether it's a pair of arborvitae in a perennial border or large architectural plants such as cardoons, you have to decide in designing your garden where the anchors will go.

Even a small garden needs strong punctuation, though it may be only one or two columnar evergreens. Large-scale anchors make the small garden seem more important, just as a big piece of furniture makes a small room more dramatic.

MIX SCALES, CREATE LAYERS IN ELEVATION

If you love tiny flowers, you can certainly have them. What you want to do is mix scales, large with small. It's fun and interesting to have an interplay of scales in a room. I always make sure there are enough big, strong pieces in a room to weight it down and give it a solid feel.

A mixture of scales gives your garden several layers of elevation. In the planning stage, when you draw elevations to visualize different garden views, aim for a staggered effect from high to low. In making elevations, the logical approach is to use the tops of trees and shrubs as different level markers. But there are other forms to consider, as well. Imagine tree trunks—their thinness or thickness, and their staggered heights—some trunks possibly very tall, and others less so. These various staggered forms all help you experience the full space of your garden.

When I bought my property in Connecticut, I inherited some very tall pines. I didn't realize at the time the gift I had been given—in essence, I didn't have to plant and wait for trees to reach mature size; I arrived to a garden roof overhead. In recent years, I have limbed up those trees and cleaned off dead and scraggly branches to show off the stand of trunks that soar like columns into the air. Those tall forms especially contribute to the excitement of the garden in winter.

Next page: An unusual border using purple, chartreuse, and lavender. The spiky euphorbia in the back illustrates the importance of strong texture in making an interesting combination of plants.

209

I've planted for staggered elevations below those majestic pines. Around the tall, strong trunks I have planted a mixture of viburnums and hydrangeas so I have blooms in the spring and at summer's end. Under the shrubs is a carpet of vinca filled with spring flowering bulbs. Even before the leaves have filled out on the shrubs, there is an early carpet of blue and yellow beneath them.

CHOOSE TO MASS PLANTS

Mass is really an aspect of scale. It's how big a visual impression a group of plants makes from a particular viewpoint. I think mass, next to large scale, is an area in which gardeners tend to be timid.

How you mass plants depends on the space you have. In a small garden, I find a large grouping of one or two things more appealing than many splotches of different plant varieties. In such a space, a pathway through just one kind of plant can be quite exciting. But the use of lots of different ground covers is confusing and makes the area seem small and cluttered. Better to resist the temptation to stick in every new plant that interests you, and opt for simplicity. If you crave variety, you can get it with bulbs or shrubs.

The scale and mass of your planting is determined by the size of your house and garden. In a small, walled urban garden, the house is still a big structure. So you've got to plant in a way that carries the scale of the house and garden wall. A large climbing hydrangea or broad spread of Boston ivy on the wall will carry the scale. A single small clematis won't. A mass of liriope on the garden floor will carry the scale. A splotch of periwinkle here and ajuga there won't.

When you do plant masses of fewer things, you're making a more architectural statement. Again, I think of another Nancy Goslee Power–designed Los Angeles garden as an illustration of this point. In a small backyard behind the modern addition to a Spanish Colonial Revival stucco house, Nancy chose to cover the ground with one plant—lavender (*Lavandula multifida*). There are numerous other plants in the garden as well—white poppies and yellow 'Mermaid' roses climbing the back wall, for example. But it is the ocean of lavender you wade into as you traverse the path that makes the strongest statement. The use of only lavender as a ground cover gives the space its unified, elegant, and utterly tranquil feeling. That yard full of purple blossoms waving in the breeze says "garden" as eloquently as the most ambitiously complex arrangement of perennials.

Over time I have learned to use mass with confidence. When I began gardening, I planted in threes (of the same variety) in my perennial borders. But the large scale of the borders required broader strokes, so now I plant in sixes or twelves. And I find more beauty in the resulting simplicity.

I have been inspired to plant in greater masses by the simple beauty of farm fields. Few sights are more unforgettable to me than the great sweeps of yellow mustard plants next to the vivid blue linseed I've seen planted in the English countryside. Just two big stripes, three feet tall. Stunning. If you've ever admired the beauty of a rolling field of American corn, you already understand the power of mass. Consider emulating the lavender fields of Provence in your Sonoma County countryside home. Your greatest stroke of gardening brilliance may be to plant a crop.

Hundreds, yes, literally hundreds, had come out in a single night; the green bushes bowed down as though they had been visited by archangels.
Katherine Mansfield, "The Garden Party," 1922[2]

I don't want to boast in advance about my grey, green, and white garden. It may be a terrible failure. . . . All the same, I cannot help hoping that the great ghostly barn-owl will sweep silently across a pale garden, next summer, in the twilight — the pale garden that I am now planting, under the first flakes of snow.
Vita Sackville-West, *The Observer*, 1950[3]

CHOOSE FOR TEXTURE

Plant texture is as much a visual pleasure as a tactile one. Think about the texture of a tapestry. Up close, the feel of a tapestry cloth may have little nuance, but from a distance the interplay of color and form gives dimension and depth.

Up close, the texture of a leaf is perceived by touch. And variegated color within one plant can give it visual texture, though its surface feels smooth. But from a distance, it's the juxtaposition of many leaf shapes and colors that expresses texture. When choosing plants for your garden, notice if the plant is big-leaved or small, delicate or bold, dainty or Amazonian.

Leaf texture is what holds a border together whether the flowers are in bloom or not, and the most interesting borders are a good mixture of textures. Plant too many similarly leaved shrubs and you've got built-in boredom. Juxtaposing a bold-leaved viburnum with a soft and fuzzy green smokebush allows each shrub to stand out. Study combinations you see and try to repeat them. It's always in combination with something else that you appreciate the texture of an individual plant.

An because a border is about texture, it's important to set it off by placing a contrasting void space with minimal texture nearby. Grass or paving work as voids.

UNIFY WITH COLOR

Color is integral to every part of a plant's aspect—from its form to its mass to its texture. And color wields considerable power in evoking mood, whether it is a sense of calm or surprise.

Ultimately, though, color is very much a personal matter. What thrills one gardener may choke another. In decorating, I try very hard to identify a client's color palette, and I think it's useful to do so in gardening, too. There is not one "correct" approach.

Personally, I love chartreuse with purple, and yellow mixed with blues and purples. I find borders that combine gray-leaved plants, pale pinks, white, and chartreuses to be pleasing. But I love hot colors, too, and a border of oranges, dark reds, and strong yellows can be just as exciting. (If you have two borders, you can do one in cool colors and the other in hot.)

UNIFY THROUGH REPETITION

There is one element of color consciousness that can benefit all gardeners and that is an awareness of the power of color to unify a garden. In my own borders, I have scattered gray-leaved plants throughout that weave together the other plantings like silver threads. You can unify lawn and beds in spring with clumps of narcissus and tulips jumping borders and popping up everywhere. Or try midsize purple alliums (large alliums with large-leaved plants) in your borders and beds. These look especially wonderful scattered throughout a mass of hostas. The allium's tall stem and round purple flower head appear to belong to the large hosta leaves, its own smaller leaves obscured. When the purple color fades, the tall stems support spiky green heads that stay the remainder of the summer, continuing to knit together large expanses of garden.

Color repetition can be done in a more systematic fashion

An orchard or any group of trees can be underplanted with one flower such as these bright red poppies for a dramatic, breathtaking effect.

The simplicity of strong rows of lavender planted in a field in Norfolk, England, are an inspiration for any garden.

I wanted to plow up all my fields and sow them with mustard after I saw meadows in England covered with the plant.

A red-stemmed saggitaria becomes sculpture in James David's Austin, Texas, garden.

A lattice obelisk creates a strong vertical element and supports the clematis and roses.

Opposite: The leaf textures and colors make the corner of this garden a fabulous spot to sit and think at the end of the day. Nicotiana sylvestris *with red orach are in complete harmony with the red roof and chair and the weathered gray fence.*

than scattering it. Consider making a checkerboard pattern with mounding plants such as golden thyme with silver-green santolina or sage. Such a display can look like a modern painting.

One- and two-color gardens can also be powerful in their unified simplicity. I've seen all-green gardens that were so magnificent they didn't need a single flower. Of course there were many greens in those gardens, subtle variations from chartreuse to the deepest black-green evergreens. An all-green scheme is an acquired taste, demanding discipline on the part of the gardener, who dares not visit a nursery in spring. I recall one serene green garden that was disrupted when a gardener lost his nerve and stuck in a few flowers.

You may never want an all-green garden, but don't feel you must integrate flower color into every part of your garden. You can mass flowers in one spot and have entirely green areas elsewhere.

SUPPORT YOUR CLIMBERS
So intently do we look down in gardening that we often fail to envision the planting possibilities offered by walls and other vertical forms. Climbing vines offer the same drama and atmosphere that the right drapes create in an interior room—they pull your eyes up to the full height of the space, and create intimacy by softening and coloring walls and openings.

Connect Architecture to Nature
Examine the wall of your house that adjoins your garden. Would it look splendid swathed in crimson Boston ivy or Virginia creeper in fall? When you cover a house or garage wall with ivy, that surface becomes one elevation of an outdoor room. And a liberal coating of ivy can also obscure an otherwise unattractive house.

Fences, trellises, arbors, and garden walls are the usual supports for vines. But how about tall metal obelisks set intermittently in a border, smothered perhaps in yellow honeysuckle? I am particularly fascinated by the tall pyramids that have a ball at the top. These strong forms, sometimes ten feet tall, add great height and form to the border and look wonderful entwined with roses or sweet potato vine. Placed intermittently, several of these can create a pleasant repetition. In my own formal garden, the four lattice columns marking the pond's corners are little gardens unto themselves; white clematis and white roses work their way up the columns each summer.

Of all the beautiful climbing possibilities, wisteria seems to evoke the strongest emotional response among gardeners (particularly those who can't grow it). If you *can* grow it, that's reason enough to build a structure for wisteria. Consider attaching a very simple pergola to your house. It creates one more roof overhead in the garden.

Let Vines Ramble and Mix with Other Plants
Vines not only look wonderful climbing up inanimate structures, they're splendid weaving through the branches of trees and working their way horizontally across low evergreen shrubs. When John Rosselli puzzled over what to do with a half-dead walnut tree on his property, he solved the dilemma by tying a wisteria to it. Because the leaves of

The wise government of space can still be found, not in Florentine modern architecture and city-planning, but in the Tuscan farmland with its enchanted economy, where every tree, every crop has its "task," of screening, shading, supporting, upholding, and grapevines wind like friezes in a graceful rope pattern among the severed elm trunks, the figs, and silvery olives.

Mary McCarthy, *The Stones of Florence*, 1959[4]

the two plants look similar, the tree took on a truly exotic appearance. An unattractive apple tree will benefit from the same treatment; climbing roses or clematis (try white *Clematis lanuginosa* 'Candida') entwined in branches will add another dimension to the tree.

Mixing climbers can produce wonderful results. Try pale yellow honeysuckle with 'Heavenly Blue' morning glories; or clematis twined with an early-blooming rose for consecutive bloomings. Also nice with clematis is purple potato vine. Or mix passionflower with jasmine.

UNDERPLANT

Ground covers are much more beautiful and natural for keeping weeds out than mulches. To reduce maintenance, I've made a point of planting ground covers at the front of my borders, using, for example, white ajuga below the white flowering plants, including viburnums and rose of Sharon. In another area I've planted masses of vinca under my viburnums for the same reason.

But underplantings include many more possibilities than the standards upon which we have come to rely, such as pachysandra and vinca. Especially when used in masses large enough to create a blanket effect, they include wildflowers, bulbs, hostas, ferns, sedums, and grasses, among others. Underplantings bring unity to a garden and make companion plants of great beauty.

Roses are particularly lovely when underplanted. One of the most fairylike combinations I've seen consisted of old-fashioned pink shrub roses underplanted with periwinkle-colored Canada phlox *(Phlox divaricata)*. And in the Peggy

Rockefeller rose garden at the New York Botanical Garden, different beds of roses are softened by underplantings of lady's mantle and helichrysum.

Also lovely are hellebores under birches and hostas under redbuds; primroses beneath apple trees; single color nasturtiums under peonies and lilies; vinca under hydrangeas; and ivy under anything.

BORDER THERAPY

You've done your border by the books. You've followed the best advice of any number of experts and have achieved some degree of all the desirable elements: colors that progress through the seasons, staggered heights from high in back to low in front, lots of different textures. Still, the composition lacks something.

My advice? You've got the basic concept down. Now start messing it up. Place some low-growing mounds midborder. Stick a few tall things in front. Make sure they're slender stems such as lilies or liatris that don't block out the view, or airy plant forms that allow you to peek through them. I use delicate *Verbena bonariensis* for this purpose; it also works as a connective thread, weaving texture throughout the whole border and unifying it with its purple color. Allow spontaneity to occur—self-seeding Johnny-jump-ups are great. These volunteers give the garden a much more natural look than when everything is precisely groomed and tortured-looking.

Look at traditional plants in new ways. If you like the bronze leaves of a canna plant but hate the pink or red flower, try cutting off the bloom when it arrives. Do you

A vine fitted by nature for the drapery of rural cottages should unite fine foliage, which holds its verdure for a long time, and is not often the prey of insects, with a good massy habit of growth. If its flowers are also beautiful or fragrant, so much the better, but by no means should fine flowers, which last for a fortnight, lead us to forget fine habit of growth and good foliage, which are constant sources of pleasure.

Andrew Jackson Downing, *The Architecture of Country Houses,* 1850[5]

The rounded boxwoods and
fritillaria create a tufted
garden in designer Jacques
Wirtz's garden in Belgium.

Green squares: simple, serene,
elegant.

love the look of red Brussels sprouts, rhubarb, asparagus, fennel, or globe artichoke in your vegetable garden? They will look equally lovely in your border; add some there, too.

Simplify. Go for stronger and fewer forms. Raise the bed if you're ambitious, but accentuate it in some way to make it stronger. Place repeated forms throughout, such as evergreens, standards, and other strong plants (cardoon, thistle, euphorbias). All of these can give rhythm to the border when repeated. If Gertrude Jekyll could use corn plants in her borders, you can use evergreens in yours. They will cut the monotony and give you something to look at when winter comes.

I visited a garden not long ago that had once been a regulation perennial border that was pretty enough but ultimately monotonous. The gardener had recently added three tall, rounded evergreens to the border. What a difference those three forms made! They created new divisions in the border and inspired the gardener to create new color schemes between the evergreens.

Landscaper Nancy McCabe has added considerable punch to her border by buttressing the whole thing. She divided it up into compartments with boxwood and made dividing lines that tapered from high in back to low in front. The new outlines change the dynamic of the border.

Such a buttressed structure could entirely change the way you plant your border. You could have one theme in each compartment—four small gardens unto themselves: vegetables in one section, flowers and herbs in others. This plan is especially great for the true plantsperson who loves collecting varieties and doesn't know where to put them.

I've done some therapy on my own perennial borders. As time has gone on, I have strengthened them by increasing their depth, and I've chosen stronger plant forms that are visible from the screened porch. I've simplified the scheme, adding more massive plantings of fewer plant types; I've raised the beds to give them more definition; and I've added vertical elements throughout the garden, all for the sake of balance and strength.

Structure in the border has an added bonus in cold climates—it creates architecture for the snow to blanket. In November I cut long evergreen boughs to make a protective cover for the border's plants, and I wrap the not-so-hardy boxwood in burlap. When I look down on the formal garden in winter, I can see the lattice, the stone wall, the evergreens, the wood pyramids, the ornaments, the boughs, and the burlap-covered box all blanketed with snow. The form is lovely unto itself, and serves as a memory of what the garden was, and what it will be again.

MIX IT UP: COMBINE RIGIDITY WITH ABANDON

For some people, "neat" and "perfect" equate with pretty, but not for me. Indoors, I want the nicks in the furniture to be visible. A living room is not a showroom. It's for living.

I feel the same aesthetic applies outdoors. A leafless lawn looks pretty sterile to me. Ditto for a perennial border groomed to within an inch of its life. I'd rather enjoy the pageant and allow the leaves to hang around for a while. And I've come to look forward to the self-seeded surprises nature builds into the border.

Plants need to be rearranged, just as furniture does from

I once knew a worthy lady who painted her house to harmonize with some magnificent rhododendrons which grew near it, and every passer-by who admired the rhododendrons blessed her unaware. Yet only around the corner, beside a house of reddish brown, was an

unhappy azalea—aflame in that crimson magenta which, as far as quarrelsomeness is concerned, carries a chip on its shoulder— and not even an evergreen between to break the violence of {the} effect. . . . Far from enjoying the blooming of the unfortunate plant, one could only be thankful when it was over.

Frances Duncan, *The Joyous Art of Gardening*, 1917[6]

time to time. Don't be intimidated by your plants—pull them up and move them around. If you don't like a section of your border, put a tarp down and pull the whole thing out to redo it. It's invigorating!

The look I love in my own garden is one of restrained abandon. Plants fall over, seedlings pop up here and there, but the tight structure of straight lines and geometrical forms pulls the garden back from the edge of chaos. The look works for me because my New England Federal house is formal, and I'm drawn to orderly spaces. But I also love profusion and abandon.

I think we worry far too much about neatness and perfection in our landscaping. If the underpinnings of your garden are strong, they will hold together the most exuberant plantings.

THRIVE WHERE YOU'RE PLANTED
If circumstance has located your prospective garden in a bog, don't let it bog you down. go with it. Make it your passion to find the best bog plants around and do something exciting with them. Whether you're interested in trees or shrubs or perennials, go walk or drive around and get a take on what really makes it. Then think about how you will arrange those plants to make them appealing, or how you will prune something to make it beautifully sculptural, or how you will mass some perennial that is usually planted in isolation or in rows. If you have been inspired by a particular garden but can't grow the exact specimens in it, find equivalents that will do the job. I can't grow Italian cypresses in my Connecticut garden but I can use arborvitae to approximate the effect. For the look of English box, I use 'Westport Blue' dwarf Korean box.

And if you love tropical plants (as I do) that don't stand a chance in your climate, pot them. I have two grand acanthus plants in urns precisely for this reason. Planted in the ground, they might look strange with their companions, but they're quite regal in isolation, elevated in containers. They summer next to the pool, then winter in the greenhouse.

In short, thrive where you're planted, as James David has done in Texas.

JAMES'S GARDEN
When landscape architect James David first moved from Louisiana to Austin, Texas, he found the landscape "a bit bleak." Accustomed to growing azaleas and camellias, he admits he made fun of cactus and yucca, but only for a short time. Soon he became fascinated by the array of unfamiliar plants his new home presented him. "I've found that whatever I make fun of, I soon embrace," says James. "It seemed right to grow things without effort."

The strong contrasts of the Texas landscape surprised and inspired him. Austin is a horticultural blend of the South and the West. While studying to be a landscape architect, he had been taught not to mix plants from disparate environments, yet he found that rule regularly violated by the land itself. Cactus thrived in hot dry spots, while inches away maidenhair ferns grew lushly in moist crevices.

The Texas landscape clearly called for a rethinking of previously held biases. Take color, for example. The Gertrude Jekyll palette of misty pastels that had once

ALOE

CACTUS

charmed him didn't stand a chance in the blazing Texas sun. Plant color has to be strong so as not to wash away in the bright light. Now he delights in using the strongest and "most bizarre" color combinations. Lime greens with burgundy. Red with dark purple. A current favorite combo includes green zinnias (*Zinnia elegans* 'Envy') with purple *Amaranthus hypochondriacus.* No color, he says, is off limits.

James David is an avid plant collector actively involved in introducing new plants into his area, and as such, he is intent upon pursuing an aesthetic that is American, and distinctly Texan. Yet he often finds inspiration for his own landscape in those he sees abroad. The rolling hills of southern France and Tuscany remind him of the hills around Austin, and the Genoan blending of desert and semi-subtropical plants—cactus cheek-by-jowl with palms—has provided a cultural context with which to compare the similar blending he encounters in Texas. More than any other influence, though, the Mediterranean tradition of growing one's own food, entertaining, and eating out-of-doors resonates most strongly for him.

James now seeks out plants with strong color, form, and texture—plants that stand up to the bright sun and sometimes stark Texas landscape. He advises other gardeners to take to heart the lesson the rocky Austin soil has taught him—to plant what thrives. "A plant has got to perform," he says, "or I'll get rid of it. I'm always finding new plants and new ideas. In other parts of the world, I'll beg, borrow, and steal ideas if they help me deal with planting in this climate. What colors my interests is the fact that this is where I live. It's about Texas."

The steps of James David's house in Texas are softened by the casual placement of hot-colored plants.

Chapter Thirteen: The Kitchen Garden

If my formal perennial borders constitute a dress-up garden where a stroll in a string of pearls might feel just right, the kitchen garden is quite the opposite. It's the garden where a city manicure quickly surrenders to country dirt, but where I find myself, nonetheless, quietly satisfied at the end of a weekend spent weeding between rows of tomatoes and snapdragons. While the formal garden aspires to the composed beauty of a still life, the kitchen one provides unbridled vitality. After twenty years of gardening, if I had to scale back and choose just one approach as my only gardening outlet, there would be no contest. My kitchen garden would win in a minute.

Anything goes in that little plot, where no two summers are quite alike. It's my experimental lab, a utilitarian source of food, a cutting garden, a repository for the overflow of plants from other gardeners and gardens, and a gathering spot for friends. It's a place where the thistle self-seeds and grows so exuberantly it dwarfs the fruit trees, yet I don't mind because it looks *interesting* to me, rather than perfect. It is, above all, a working garden where I pot, weed, plant, and harvest.

The kitchen garden is laid out in a "four-square" plan that is as old as the Middle Ages. It is an enclosed space, which makes it very intimate, fenced on three sides, with a barn serving as the fourth wall. Along the north side of the garden fence stretches a pergola with chairs and a bench beneath it. Divided into four equal rectangles, the garden is intersected by crossing paths and planted with rows of vegetables, herbs, and flowers. Around the perimeter of the fence is a border where I grow perennials. Fruit trees

An intimate kitchen garden.

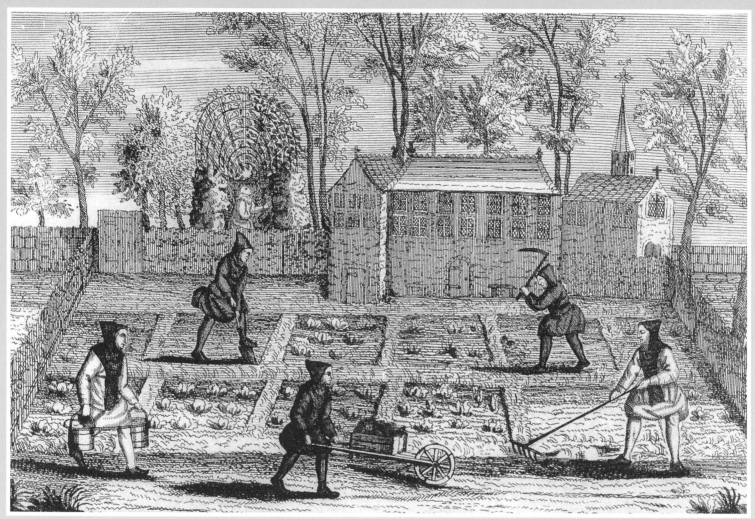

Artist unknown, Monks Working in a Garden, *14th century. Bibliothèque Nationale, Paris.*

Kitchen gardens are the earliest of all gardens—food being somewhat more central for survival than flowers.

punctuate the beds and balance one side of the garden with the pergola opposite them.

MAINTENANCE

Among the chief virtues of a kitchen garden is its user-friendly format. Surely the reason the kitchen garden's form—squares and rectangles intersected by paths—has varied so little over the years is the simplicity of upkeep that comes from such a design. Because one gardens in beds, one can mulch to keep weeds at a minimum. I use salt hay, a very fine, biodegradable option that is quite pretty. And since plants are arranged in rows, they can be staked in a much more severe way than you would if you had the same things in a perennial border. A row of tall dahlias can be held upright with a couple of bamboo sticks and long string as opposed to individual supports for plants scattered throughout the borders. Rows also allow you to get in and out easily to do your weeding.

I tend to plant very densely, which cuts down on maintenance, but a half hour with a weeder between rows every other day will keep the beds looking neat. Because of the rigid planting, though, you can't let a kitchen garden go. The beds must be kept very precise, unlike some other schemes that can take care of themselves during brief periods of neglect.

I don't regard this fact as discouraging, however. I love going out with a glass of iced tea to look after the pots in the afternoon, and to deadhead and loosen up the soil in the beds. Inevitably someone shows up and he or she is soon deadheading right along with me.

One to rot and one to grow,
One for the pigeon and one for the crow.
Old English planting rhyme

Fertilizing the soil for the following year is part of the garden's cycle. I use my own compost and top dress the beds every fall with well-rotted manure. A kitchen garden's soil needs to be kept very rich. You're asking annual plants to do everything in one season—grow and produce flowers and vegetables—so you need to enrich the earth regularly. And because I use different planting patterns each year, the net effect is that I'm rotating my crops and not depleting the soil of the same nutrients on a regular basis.

LOCATING THE GARDEN

You can locate a kitchen garden anywhere you have full sun. Historically, such gardens often were located close to the house so a cook could easily pick the freshest herbs for dinner. Nancy McCabe situated hers at the entrance to her house, so visitors walk past wonderful espaliered apple trees and vegetables when paying a call. Whether it's on the back, front, or side of your house, it should be a place that you go through all the time.

Because my house is surrounded by shade, I located my kitchen garden near an old barn that anchors it on one side. Before I broke ground, I looked to the barn for clues about appropriate structural materials to use, as you might look to your house for clues. I also worked on getting the proportions of the kitchen garden to relate to the barn's proportions. This balance was ultimately achieved by eyeing different dimensions rather than defining them on graph paper. I took wooden stakes and string and moved the lines around until I found an appropriate size. My vegetable garden ended up being forty-five by sixty-five

SCARECROW

George Washington's Virginia home, Mount Vernon, has a large plot that holds fruit trees, vegetables, and flowers in a lovely walled space.

The tall simple poles placed for supports throughout Thomas Jefferson's vegetable garden at Monticello give a sense of architecture in the open space.

feet, but kitchen gardens can be much smaller or larger and still remain completely engaging. If you're serious about feeding a family of four from the garden, however, you should opt for a bigger plot than I currently have.

PLANTING

The kitchen garden is where I like to try out seeds and new plants, to observe their growing habits before they get put into other gardens. It's also home to the old standards that are required summer eating: basil, tomatoes, lettuces, and sugar snap peas, or the hard-to-get favorites like white eggplant, sorrel, and arugula. I grow red Swiss chard, kale, fennel, and cabbage, too, not only to eat but to cut and include in flower arrangements. I've found I tend to grow more flowers than vegetables, since the farmer down the road can grow many space-taking plants like corn much better than I can. That's one of the hard decisions a gardener with limited space or sun must make.

Some of the best gardening fun I have is in winter when I plan a new planting scheme for spring. I plot out the design on graph paper, taking into account the mature sizes of plants. In the past, I've arranged things by pattern and by texture; this year, color won out as the dominant theme. Two of the beds were designated for hot colors—reds and yellows—while the other two got cool pinks and blues. All are edged with parsley. For continuity, I added purple-leaved plants throughout all four beds, and plants with silver foliage in most of the pots. The rhythmic repetition of these colors knits together the whole composition.

Sometimes the patterned effects produced by using

The number of forms, mazes and knots is so great . . . that I leave every housewife to herself . . . and note this generally, that all plots are square, and all are bordered with privit, raisins, fea-berries, roses, thorn, rosemary, bee-flowers, hyssop, sage or such like.

William Lawson, *The Countrie Housewife's Garden*, 1617[1]

different colors of lettuce can resemble medieval knot gardens—so beautiful, in fact, that you don't want to pick the lettuce. My solution to the dilemma has been to plant two rows of lettuces close together; in that way, I can harvest some and still enjoy the picture. I do the same with kale and cabbages. Still, you have to accept that your lovely patterns will have holes in time, and that's why it's so useful to have some structural underpinnings in a kitchen garden.

THE STYLISH KITCHEN GARDEN

As humble as a kitchen garden may be, planted with rows of utilitarian food choices and flowers for cutting, there's no reason it can't be wonderfully stylish. The mood may be dressed down and casual, but it can incorporate all the elements of style you might lavish upon a more formal garden. In fact, I think my kitchen plot is the prettiest garden I have because it is the most loved. It's certainly the garden everyone seems to prefer.

I have found that the same understandings about structure that I've used elsewhere are entirely relevant in the kitchen garden. Here's a quick list of suggestions for creating a garden that appeals to your sense of design as well as your appetite:

Use geometry on the floor of the garden. There's nothing like tight structure to hold together a planting scheme that by its very nature is exuberant. You can use squares, rectangles, and triangles to keep some form. For herbs, consider experimenting with some of the wonderful knot patterns available.

KNOT PATTERN HERB GARDEN

Enclose the space. The obvious reason is to keep hungry deer and rabbits at bay. But you enjoy the benefits of a fence in a kitchen garden as elsewhere. Roses and clematis grow on mine, with espaliered pear trees on the outside. The fence also serves as a backdrop for narrow beds of tall annuals and perennials for cutting. I grow dahlias, peonies, and hollyhocks there, plus the spillover plants from the formal garden. The fence imparts a roomlike quality to the area, a certain coziness I feel when I'm out there picking tomatoes.

Choose building materials that suit the site and mood. I took my clues for fence materials from the adjoining barn. At a lumberyard, I found some weathered boards that had been left outside. Chicken wire, right in keeping with the mood of the barn, has been added to keep hungry critters out.

Add a charming path. Old moss-covered brick pavers do the job here, adding tons of character to a simple scheme. If your garden has stone or brick paths, the maintenance is even lower than grass paths, which must be mowed. I've found you can cut down on the amount of ground surface that has to be kept up by adding more pathways.

Make a friendly entrance. The entrance doesn't have to be fancy. I've used an old gate decorated with interesting hinges, but all kinds of possibilities will make the kitchen garden inviting to guests. Consider an arbor, or an antique wrought-iron gate, or a contemporary one made by a local craftsman.

Use decorative staking and edging materials. Who says those ugly tomato cages are the best way to support your Early Girls? I have five-foot tepees of willow branches for my climbing sweet peas, and bamboo stakes for the tomatoes. A border of parsley or nasturtiums or nepeta will do fine around the edges of beds, but for added definition, I've lined them with charcoal-colored Victorian rope tiles. You may want to try bricks set on edge, or running hoops made from twigs or metal.

Pull the eye up with vertical elements. In the kitchen garden, as in the perennial border, it's nice to invite the sky into the picture. Do this by planting shapely fruit trees and adding tall metal forms as supports for vines. I have pairs of dwarf Korean lilac standards and viburnum standards clipped into balls. Rusted metal obelisks support deep purple sweet potato vines and look wonderful in August. I use plant stands for pots throughout the garden, too. They bring fragrant, low-growing favorites like fringed dianthus and auriculas, which tend to get lost in the beds, up to nose level. Even when they're not on stands, though, plants elevated only a foot high off the ground in pots offer another elevation in the staggered low-to-high height progression.

Don't forget the pots. It may seem redundant to add potted plants to a kitchen garden, almost like gilding the lettuce, but some plants do much better in pots. Anything that needs to winter over in the greenhouse gets the pot treatment, from lime trees to fuchsia and datura standards to aloe plants. Some herbs, too, are happier in pots. And invasive herbs like mint and lemon balm will

WIRE STAKING CAGE

BAMBOO STAKING FORM

Paths of antique brick separate the beds in my kitchen garden, which I based on a medieval plan.

The herb garden at Boscobel gardens in New York employs the medieval plan that I also used.

stay put in a pot. All of these plants can be rotated and moved for best sun exposure because they're portable.

Sometimes it's fun just to give an ordinary but very pretty vegetable, like cabbage or Swiss chard, the star treatment by placing it in a pot on a stand. I use pairs of potted heliotrope standards to mark the beginning of each path. Their delicious fragrance wafts through the garden when I brush past them.

Use ornament here, too. Once you've established the basic structure of your garden, it's fun to layer on details that enhance the kitchen garden's sense of intimacy. Besides the old lightning bolt at the center, I've added other artifacts. Bell jars and rhubarb forcers work hard in the spring, but stay out for the rest of the season. Other functional items are decorative, too. The hose nozzle is a bronze rabbit, for example, and the watering cans, which sit out all summer, are a pretty collection of shapes. Anything visible in this small garden is made to look appealing.

Make a comfortable place to sit and enjoy the view. You may go to your kitchen garden to work, but you'll stay if it's as pretty as other gardens. So find a spot to locate a chair or two, preferably in a shady area. I've managed this by constructing a pergola at the end of the garden. There I've put some of my favorite garden seats—rusted but serviceable fern chairs and a wooden bench—which are in keeping with the casual mood of the garden. The rustic pergola makes a nice visual transition from the organized kitchen garden to the natural woodland area nearby.

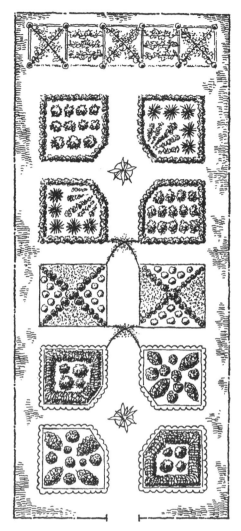

RECTANGULAR GARDEN PLAN

CIRCULAR GARDEN PLAN

Rows and rows of red lettuce are held in tightly by a hedge of
boxwood and surrounded by rampant-growing pumpkins.

CHAPTER FOURTEEN: MAINTENANCE

In a garden, things grow.

Jerzy Kosinski, *Being There*, 1971[1]

When it comes to garden maintenance, the comparison of outdoor and indoor rooms quickly falls apart. Indoors, your seven-foot sofa won't grow to eight, your chairs don't get mold and Japanese beetles, your rugs won't sprout dandelions. Your living room, unless it's regularly visited by children and animals, can survive with a weekly vacuuming and dusting. It can even go two weeks without showing signs of neglect. Try that in a garden.

Any seasoned gardener knows the real truth: Ignore your garden for a couple of weeks and all hell breaks loose. That's why, before you install a fifty-foot perennial border, it's important to do a reality check.

Just how much time *can* you devote to gardening each week? Gardens are about change and growth. But some gardens change less than others. If you can only commit to brief bouts of upkeep, it's important from the beginning to plan a garden for yourself and those who will share it that is realistic, and that won't fall to ruin after one season.

BUILD IN SIMPLICITY WITH STRUCTURE

There are a number of approaches that can give you the pleasure of a garden with very little upkeep required. By building low maintenance into the garden plan, you can enjoy your garden on the weekend, free of guilt.

The Living Wall Garden

I'm talking here about a hedge surrounding a square or rectangle of grass and one bench. Sound stark? Chauncey Stillman's Wethersfield has just such a garden room and it's one of the most tranquil spots in New York State. Granted,

It is so handy to leave all the tools, pots, and fertilizers you need for the maintenance of your garden in one space, as in my potting shed.

Next page: In a part of this property that might have gone unnoticed, Robert Dash has created a most unusual garden by scattering rounded boxwoods among the trees.

Wethersfield's arborvitae hedges are now quite old and soar about twenty feet up, but inside it is a piece of heaven, with no other plantings save for a grass floor. Hate mowing grass? Then make the floor gravel. Total time commitment: one annual pruning and one fertilizing of the hedge, plus an occasional rake of the gravel.

Italian gardens are wonderful models for this approach. Hedges, stone paving, a comfortable chair, and some stone ornament—a small trickling fountain, perhaps. Add an ornamental specimen tree for shape and shade. That's all it takes, because the unchanging permanent elements spell "garden" as clearly as a truckload of hollyhocks.

The Walled Garden

A variation on this theme is the courtyard or garden walled with masonry. In a climate that's warm year-round, enclose a gravel courtyard with a pink or orange stucco wall next to your modern house. For a graphically beautiful effect, silhouette plants with strong form against the wall—cactus or euphorbia. Add a couple of agaves in huge pots. Total commitment: very occasional raking of gravel and watering of plants.

The Grove

Plant an orchardlike grid of fruit trees such as apples or pears or a more informal scattering of birch trees. Underplant it with ground cover—periwinkle or santolina under the birches; white ajuga under the fruit trees. Scatter narcissus and tulips throughout the area for spring color. Total time commitment: annual fertilizing and pruning of trees, occasional weeding of ground cover as it gets established.

The Container Garden

Container gardens are low maintenance if you plant them simply. Better to put single plants in individual containers and arrange the pots rather than trying to make a mini-perennial garden in one large pot. When a plant fails, just remove the pot and add something later.

PLANT SIMPLY

Simplicity always wins the day in a low-maintenance garden. Plant a border thick with hostas instead of perennial and annual flowers. Avoid having little patches of plantings here and there. Make fewer, stronger statements in the landscape, but always do it with the underlying structure in mind.

PLANT WHAT THRIVES

Coddling marginal plants through a cold winter takes time. It's rewarding if you have help or the hours to do it yourself, but truly silly if you don't. Use plants that succeed in your climate and soil.

PREPARE YOUR SOIL PROPERLY

Whether you are planting a rose, shrub, tomato, or oak tree, proper soil preparation will save you later fuss as you try to rescue a plant that's failing to thrive. The information is available; do your homework. If you're uncertain about the acidity of your soil, you can have it tested professionally.

For the last forty years of my life I have broken my back, my finger-nails, and sometimes my heart, in the practical pursuit of my favorite occupation.

Vita Sackville-West, *The Observer*[2]

Just Say No to Pine Bark

Commercially available mulches are real time-savers that keep weeds down, but some are prettier than others. My pet peeve: big chunks of ugly pine bark that currently threaten to blanket the United States. I prefer a double- or triple-shred bark mulch that is very fine and looks like rich humus when scattered under shrubs. Though it needs to be added to yearly since it decomposes, it retains the earth's moisture. Cocoa hulls are also pretty, though they look less natural and set off some real cognitive dissonance when you bend over to have a look at your peonies and get a whiff of chocolate. The smell eventually wears off, though.

Underplant, Underplant, Underplant

Ground covers, once established, are real labor-savers; they retain moisture and choke out weeds. Plant carpets of ajuga, vinca, thyme, sedums. Try strawberries or nasturtiums.

Plant Densely

Try not to leave too much bare soil in a perennial border or vegetable garden. Plant things cheek by jowl. I find it hurts less to thin out desirable plants than to pull weeds.

Stake Early On

At the beginning of spring, when the first perennials pop up after a long winter, I stick apple tree branches saved from winter pruning near the plants when they are about a foot tall. I use branches that are two to three feet high. The plants then grow up through the little structure and entwine themselves in the twigs.

The branches offer the new plants just enough extra support so that in July and August they won't flop over. The plants retain a natural growing habit in this way. If I don't do early staking and later things do fall over, staking them at that point creates a very artificial look.

If you don't have your own apple trees, other twiglike branches will do. Or visit a nearby orchard at pruning time.

Use Natural Materials for Stakes

I love delphiniums and stake them when they get battered down by a hard rain. For these I use natural bamboo cane and raffia ties rather than green plastic stakes with twist ties. Visible man-made staking materials in a natural setting ruin the picture for me. There is one exception— pantyhose. Yes, old pantyhose, sliced into rings. They make flexible and invisible ties for tomatoes and roses.

For the cutting garden, annuals can be staked more rigidly than they are in a mixed border. That doesn't mean they can't be pretty. I use bamboo sticks crisscrossed on each side of the plants.

I also place short stakes in a row with twine tied from each stake to make low supports. Use taller stakes to train beans or short vines.

For tomato staking, I had tall, strong stakes cut that I reuse every year. These not only hold up the plant, they add lovely architecture to the vegetable garden.

Five-foot-high pyramids of long cleaned branches, circled with twine, soon become swathed with vines each year in my kitchen garden. There's a pyramid in each of two sections, balancing each other, and adding height and form.

LOOPED WILLOW STAKING

WILLOW STAKING WITH TWINE

SIMPLE WILLOW STAKING

A grid of bamboo stakes creates a natural architectural frame for this stand of delphiniums and prevents the stems from falling over.

Rings of natural willow surrounding short stakes hold the peonies upright but blend in with the plant material.

My wife had no garden clothes . . . When she paid a call on her perennial borders . . . she merely wandered out into the cold and wet, into the sun and warmth, wearing whatever she had put on that morning. . . . If when she arrived back indoors the Ferragamos were encased in muck, she kicked them off. If the tweed suit was a mess, she sent it to the cleaners.

E. B. White, in the introduction to Katharine White's *Onward and Upward in the Garden,* 1979[3]

Early staking is essential in the maintenance of a garden, where willow bows tied to a locust post give support for summer vines.

Potting sheds can be picturesque in a garden corner.

Ask a Japanese gardener the secret of gardening and he will hold up his pruning shears.

Teijo Ito, *The Japanese Garden*, 1972[4]

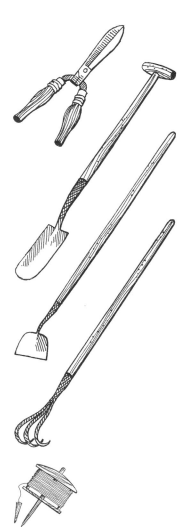

TOOLS

In addition to the tools everyone needs for gardening—shovel, hoe, and pruner—here are a few things I find I can't live without (some are harder to find than others):

· Narrow spade: Because it causes little damage to neighboring roots, this is ideal for transplanting in existing borders.

· Cultivator with long handle: I use this for the back of borders and kitchen rows.

· Heart-shaped hoe: This pointed hoe makes great rows for seeds. I then use it to cover them up.

· Marker with cord.

· Sharp Felco pruners: These are always near the back door or in my pocket.

· Other helpful items: An underground watering hose. Black rubber hoses seep water and are nearly invisible even when they're above ground. Buried sprinkling systems are also useful and the cost is not prohibitive if you install them yourself.

Another great investment is a mulcher. Every twig and leaf you take up off your property can go back to the earth as ground-up mulch for top-dressing shrubs. You can do this once in the spring and once in fall as part of your seasonal cleanup. Keep it out of sight in your garage.

Make It Fun

On the garden neatness scale, my tastes fall somewhere between perfection and abandon. I want to nurture my garden and to have it look well kept, yet I want self-seeding nature to have enough elbow room. And so I try to keep the two inclinations in balance.

Help with garden chores allows me the luxury of a big formal garden and a vegetable garden, too. Still, on weekends, there are weeds to be pulled. And so I try to make it fun. I weed and chat with friends. Weed and walk the dogs. Weed and have a glass of wine. Weed for the sheer senselessness of it.

When I've arranged my little patch of the earth to my liking, and gaze about to find, incredibly, that I'm surrounded by madly blooming plants, I feel that all is right with the world. And that's precisely why I garden.

Utilitarian equipment can also be a beautiful accent in a garden.

What better way to get over a black mood than an hour of furious weeding! That violent tearing up and casting away of the dreadfully healthy weeds also tears up and casts away the dreadfully healthy demons.

May Sarton, *Plant Dreaming Deep,* 1968[5]

V

THE GARDENER IN WINTER

CHAPTER FIFTEEN: FIRESIDE GARDENING

If we had no winter, the spring
would not be so pleasant;
if we did not sometimes taste of adversity,
prosperity would not be so welcome.

Anne Bradstreet, *Meditations Divine and Moral,* 1664[1]

Winter in Connecticut is not a time of discontent for me. From November through April my gardening downtime is filled with reading, planning, reflection, and anticipation. Weekends are spent by a fire, with plant catalogs, magazines, tour brochures, and gardening books piled around me.

It's a winter habit I developed years ago when I lived in a New York apartment and so wanted a garden. My friend Mike McCabe, the owner of Lion's Head Books in Salisbury, Connecticut, introduced me to the writings of Vita Sackville-West and Gertrude Jekyll. Another dear friend, the late Timothy Mawson, opened the world of Jekyll's architect/collaborator Edwin Lutyens to me. Slowly I have accumulated a library of cherished gardening titles.

So many wonderful resources are available to gardeners today, not the least of which is the amazing array of catalogs now in print. Wanting more unusual plant material comes with the territory once you're hooked on gardening. And depending on where you live, catalogs may have to be your main source for those unusual things. Following this chapter are some favorite sources for plants from all over the country. Many of the catalogs are as much fun to read as the plants are fun to receive. Remember one thing when you order: The plants will be small. I sometimes put them in rows in the kitchen garden for a season before I put them in the borders.

GARDEN TOURS
In my design career, nothing has done as much for my development as traveling and looking at every great house

A bird's nest and Christmas evergreens fill the empty plant stand during the winter.

I could get myself into. Whether in Charleston, South Carolina, or Jaipur, India, I have found lessons I could carry home with me.

Public and private gardens are of equal value to the gardener. Start locally with garden club tours and a visit to the nearest botanical garden. Find any public gardens nearby. Some may be a part of a historic house.

There is another resource with which we are blessed here in the United States. The Garden Conservancy, based in Cold Spring, New York, was founded to ensure the preservation and care of great gardens in this country. A few years ago, the conservancy began publishing an Open Days Directory for the Connecticut, New York, and New Jersey areas; now the directory has been expanded to include gardens throughout the country. For a small fee, Garden Conservancy members as well as nonmembers can tour private gardens on their respective open days from May through September.

This tradition comes to us from England, where gardens are often open to the public. I remember once walking through a village in the Cotswolds and seeing a sign leaning up against a hedge that read GARDEN OPEN DAY. Next to it was a small box where you could leave a shilling or two. The garden was enchanting.

There's nothing more valuable to a gardener than to see how other accomplished gardeners do it. Especially instructive are the gardens that are tended entirely by the owner. This gives you an idea of what's reasonably doable in your own space.

And the gardens you visit shouldn't be restricted only to those nearby. I may not be able to grow the euphorbias I see on the West Coast, yet I can still learn by seeing how Californians deal with space, arrange plants, and create vistas and interest in their gardens. When you're out of your own community, perhaps abroad, and not sure where to look for a guide to garden tours, go to a bookstore or library first and ask for one.

Following are some of the books and catalogs I've found most useful in making my garden, along with plant lists, great public gardens and directories for private ones, and sources for garden supplies.

Announced by all the trumpets of the sky,
arrives the snow.

Ralph Waldo Emerson, "The Snowstorm"[2]

254

Selected Gardens

BLOEDEL RESERVE
7571 N.E. Dolphin Drive
Bainbridge Island, WA 98110-1097
(206) 842-7631

BOSCOBEL RESTORATION
Route 9D
Garrison-on-Hudson, NY 10524
(914) 265-3638

CENTRAL PARK CONSERVANCY GARDEN
(at 105th and 5th Avenue)
Managed by the Central Park Conservancy
The Arsenal, Central Park
New York, NY 10021
(212) 315-0385

CHICAGO BOTANIC GARDEN
1000 Lake Cook Road
P.O. Box 400
Glencoe, IL 60022-0400
(847) 835-5440

DUMBARTON OAKS
1703 32nd St. N.W.
Washington, D.C. 20007
(202) 339-6400

FAIRCHILD TROPICAL GARDENS
10901 Old Cutler Road
Miami, FL 33156
(305) 667-1651

FILOLI
Canada Road
Woodside, CA 94062
(415) 364-8300

HUNTINGTON
BOTANICAL GARDENS
1151 Oxford Road
San Marino, CA 91108
(818) 405-2100

INNISFREE
Tyrrel Road
Millbrook, NY 12545
(914) 677-8000

KYKUIT ESTATE TOURS
150 White Plains Road
Tarrytown, NY 10591
(914) 631-9491

LADEW TOPIARY GARDENS
3535 Jarrettsville
Monkton, MD 21111
(410) 557-9466

LONGWOOD GARDENS
(30 miles west of Philadelphia;
3 miles northeast of Kennett Square)
P.O. Box 501
Kennett Square, PA 19348
(610) 388-1000, (800) 737-5500

MONTICELLO
Route 53
Charlottesville, VA 22902
(804) 984-9800

MORVEN FARM
Ellerslie Farm Office
3201 Ellerslie Drive
Charlottesville, VA 22902
(804) 293-3978

MOUNT VERNON
Mount Vernon, VA 22121
(703) 780-2000

NAUMKEAG
Prospect Hill Road
P.O. Box 792
Stockbridge, MA 01262
(413) 298-3239

PACA GARDEN
1 Martin Street
Annapolis, MD 21401
(410) 267-6656

STAN HYWET HALL AND GARDENS
714 N. Portage Street
Akron, OH 44303
(330) 836-5533

TRYON PALACE HISTORIC SITES & GARDENS
610 Pollock St.
P.O. Box 1007
New Bern, NC 28563
(919) 514-4900

VIZCAYA MUSEUM AND GARDENS
3251 South Miami Avenue
Miami, FL 33129
(305) 250-9133

WAVE HILL
West 249th Street and Independence Avenue
(Right off Henry Hudson Parkway)
New York, NY 10471
(718) 549-2055, (718) 549-3200

WESTBURY GARDENS
P.O. Box 430
Old Westbury, NY 11568
(516) 333-0048

WETHERSFIELD FARM
(7 miles northeast of Millbrook, NY)
Write c/o
Wethersfield House
RR1, Box 444
Amenia, NY 12501
(914) 373-8037

WINTERTHUR
(6 miles northwest of Wilmington, DE)
Winterthur, DE 19735
(800) 448-3883

GARDEN GUIDES

THE GARDEN CONSERVANCY
OPEN DAYS DIRECTORY
P.O. Box 219
Cold Spring Harbor, NY 10516
(914) 265-2029
*This guide lists private gardens across the country
that will be open on specific days.*

THE GARDEN TOURIST
by Lois G. Rosenfeld
The Garden Tourist Press
330 West 72nd Street
New York, NY 10023
(212) 874-6211
Fax (212) 799-7094
*A guide, organized by state, to garden events (tours,
shows, plant sales, and special events; some international
event information)*

THE NATIONAL GARDENS SCHEME
(YELLOW BOOK)
Hatchlands Park
East Clandon, Guildford, Surrey GU4 7RT
*For gardens in England, Wales and Scotland,
a directory of public gardens and a listing of "open days"
for private ones.*

PLANT LISTS

PLANTS FOR HEDGES, MAKING WALLS, AND BUILDING ROOMS

LATIN NAME, COMMON NAME:

Berberis spp., Barberries
Buxus spp., Boxwood
Carpinus spp., Hornbeams
Euonymus spp.
Ilex crenata, Japanese hollies
Ligustrum, Privet
Myrica pensylvanica, Bayberry
Rosa spp.
Taxus spp., Yews
Tsuga, Hemlock
Viburnum spp.

PLANTS FOR ARCHITECTURAL INTEREST

LATIN NAME, COMMON NAME:

Agave spp.
Allium spp.
Angelica Archangelica
Angelica gigas
Astilboides tabularis, Poor man's gunnera
Beta vulgaris, Rhubarb chard
Columnar evergreens
Crambe cordifolia
Eremurus spp.
Euphorbia spp.
Gunnera manicata
Ligularia spp.
Macleaya cordata, Plume poppy
Nicotiana sylvestris
Onopordum Acanthium, Scotch thistle
Peltiphyllum peltatum, Umbrella plant
Petasites japonicus
Rheum spp., Ornamental rhubarbs
Rodgersia spp.

PLANTS FOR LEAF COLOR: BRONZE/BURGUNDY

LATIN NAME, COMMON NAME:

Acer palmatum spp., Japanese maples
Alternanthera dentata 'Rubiginosa'
Amaranthus erythrostachys
Angelica gigas
Berberis thunbergii 'Crimson Pygmy'
Berberis thunbergii 'Rosy Glow'
Beta vulgaris, Rhubarb chard
Cotinus 'Royal Robe', Purple smokebush
Cotinus 'Velvet Cloak, Purple smokebush
Euphorbia amygdaloides 'Purpurca'
Heuchera 'Palace Purple'
Heuchera 'Pewter Veil'
Heuchera 'Stormy Seas'
Hibiscus Acetosella
Ipomoea batatas 'Blackie', Black sweet-potato vine
Lysimachia ciliata 'Purpurea', Red money
Mikania dentata, Brazilian haze vine
Pennisetum setaceum 'Burgundy Giant'
Penstemon digitalis 'Husker's Red'
Perilla frutescens 'Atropurpurea', Shiso
Prunus x *cistena,* Sand cherry
Ricinus communis 'Sanguineus', Castor bean

PLANTS FOR LEAF COLOR: CHARTREUSE / GOLD

LATIN NAME, COMMON NAME:

Alchemilla spp.
Amaranthus caudatus 'Green Tails'
Berberis x *Bonanza Gold*
Beta vulgaris 'Golden'
Euphorbia spp.
Helichrysum petiolare 'Limelight'
Hosta 'August Moon'
Hosta x 'Piedmont Gold'
Humulus lupulus 'Aureus', Golden hops
Ipomoea batatas 'Margarita', Green sweet potato
Kochia scoparia 'Childsii'
Moluccella laevis 'Bells of Ireland'
Nicotiana langsdorfii
Nicotiana x *sanderae* 'Nikki hybrid' or 'Lime Green'
Robinia pseudoacacia 'Frisia', Golden locust
Sagina subulata 'Aurea', Gold Irish moss
Spiraea x *Bumalda* 'Lime Mound'
Spiraea japonica 'Goldflame'
Zinnia elegans 'Envy'

PLANTS FOR LEAF COLOR: GRAY

LATIN NAME, COMMON NAME:

Athyrium nipponicum 'Pictum', Japanese painted fern
Buddleia alternifolia 'Argentea'
Caryopteris spp.
Convolvulus cneorum
Cynara cardunculus, Cardoon
Eryngium spp.
Eryngium giganteum
Fothergilla gardenii 'Blue Mist'
Helichrysum angustifolium, Curry plant
Helichrysum petiolare
Hosta sieboldiana 'Elegans'
Larix
Lotus berthelotii
Macleaya cordata, Plume poppy
Perovskia atriplicifolia, Russian sage
Plectranthus argentatus
Pyrus salicifolia 'Pendula'
Rosa rubrifolia
Salix elaeagnus
Salix purpurea 'Nana'
Salix purpurea 'Pendula'
Salvia discolor
Stachys byzantina 'Helen von Stein', Big ears
Teucrium fruticans
Verbascum bombyciferum
Westringia rosmariniformis

PLANTS FOR FOCAL POINTS OR LIVING ORNAMENTS

LATIN NAME, COMMON NAME:

Acer palmatum spp., Japanese maples
Brugmansia innoxia, Angel's trumpet
Buxus spp., Boxwood
Chionanthus virginicus, Fringe tree
Fagus sylvatica f. *purpurea*, Copper beech
Hydrangea panniculata 'Grandiflora', Tree hydrangea
Lilac standards
Magnolia spp.
Palms
Picea glauca 'conica' Dwarf alberta spruce
Pyrus salicifolia 'Pendula', Weeping pear
Rheum spp., Ornamental rhubarbs
Rosemary standard
Salix purpurea 'Nana'
Stewartia pseudocamellia

PLANTS FOR GROUNDCOVER OR FLOORING

LATIN NAME, COMMON NAME:

Ajuga spp.
Asarum spp., Gingers
Chamomile
Convallaria, Lily-of-the-valley
Epimedium spp.
Ferns
Galium ordoratum, Sweet Woodruff
Helleborus spp.
Liriope spp., Lilyturf
Mentha requienii, Corsican mint
Mosses
Myosotis, Forget-me-nots
Nasturtium
Nepeta spp., Catmints
Phlox stolonifera
Sagina sublata, Irish moss
Sedum spp.
Sempervivum spp.
Thymus spp.
Vinca minor

Plants for Draping, Vining, and Climbing

Latin Name, Common Name:

Actinidia spp., Kiwi vine
Akebia quinata
Aristolochia spp., Dutchman's-pipe
Asarina spp.
Cardiospermum halicacabum, Love-in-a-puff
Clematis spp.
Cobaea scandens, Cup-and-saucer vine
Humulus spp., Hops
Hydrangea anomala var. *petiolaris,* Climbing hydrangea
Ipomoea spp., Morning glories
Jasminum, Jasmine
Mandevilla spp.
Pandora jasminoides
Passiflora spp., Passionflowers
Plumbago auriculata
Rhodochiton atrosanguineum, Purple bell vine
Rosa spp.
Solanum jasminoides, Potato vine
Solanum spp.
Wisteria spp.

CONTAINER PLANTING SCHEMES

Cathie Denckla offers the following five planting schemes for large containers.

PLANTING SCHEME 1
(for eighteen-inch terra-cotta pot)

This planting scheme uses plants with different textures and growing habits, unified by the colors.

Silver marguerite daisy, double form
(*Argyranthemum frutescens* 'Foeniculaceum')
White flower; wispy, fernlike leaves; bushy, multi-branched form; soft-looking

Variegated iris (*Iris pallida* 'Aurea Variegata')
White and green foliage with blue flower; short lived, but the vertical, strong, smooth leaves stay erect all summer

Variegated felicia daisy (*Felicia anelloides* 'Variegata')
Green and creamy yellow leaf; blue flower with yellow center; low and branching with small leaves and flowers; shoots off sides of pot

Lobelia (*Lobelia pendula* 'White Cascade')
White flower; soft, cascading, trailing over edge of pot

Golden sage (*Salvia officinalis* 'Aurea Variegata')
Green with yellow-green edge; wonderful textured leaf; bushy and compact

Violet (*Viola* 'Blueberries and Cream')
Blue and cream (who can resist those faces!); when shaded by other stronger plants, it will pop its head up all summer

Variegated ivy (*Hedera helix* 'Good Child')
Green with yellow edge; cascading, smooth leaf

Coleus (*Coleus blumei* 'Black Dragon')
Deep, deep blackish purple; velvety leaf; dramatic—stops the eye

PLANTING SCHEME 2
(grasses in container)

Plant these grasses together, set them by flowing water, and watch the composition move!

Variegated Japanese silver grass *(Miscanthus sinensis* 'Variegatus'*)*

Japanese blood grass *(Imperata cylindrica* 'Rubra'*)*

Golden Japanese forest grass *(Hakonechloa macra* 'Aureola'*)*

PLANTING SCHEME 3

Love-in-a-mist *(Nigella damascena* 'Miss Jekyll')
Pale blue flowers; the soft and frilly plant produces wonderful seedpods after its blooms have faded (don't cut them off— they move in the breeze)

White geranium *(Geranium* 'Pinto')
An ordinary geranium with wonderful blooms

Salvia *(Salvia coccinea* 'Brenthurst')
Peachy pink spikes

Coral bells *(Heuchera* 'Palace Purple')
Small white flowers, but the bronze leaves, shaped like small lily pads, are the real beauty of this plant

Oregano *(Origanum* 'Kentish Beauty')
Silver green leaves make trailing whorls over the pot's edge

Helichrysum *(Helichrysum petiolare)*
Soft and fuzzy silver foliage

Verbena *(Verbena* x h. 'Stirling Star')
Pale lavender; finely cut leaves that trail or climb

Lobelia *(Lobelia erinus compacta* 'Cambridge Blue')
Cascading blue flowers

Purple sage *(Salvia officinalis* 'Purpurea')
Purple/green, textured leaves

PLANTING SCHEME 4
(for twenty-inch pot)

This scheme also uses varied textures and growing habits but draws its charm from a cooler, more limited color palette.

Cosmos (*Cosmos bipinnatus* 'Sonata')
White flower; tall, wispy, fine foliage that blows in the breeze

Salvia (*Salvia coccinea* 'Snow Nymph')
White flowers along stiff spires

Cotton lavender *(Santolina chamaecyparissus {syn. S. incana})*
Dainty, aromatic, soft silver mounds

White maidens pinks (*Dianthus deltoides* 'Albus')
White flowers; grey, grasslike foliage, which lasts after flowers finish; low, spreading habit; spicy scent

Black mondo grass (*Ophiopogon planiscapus* 'Ebony')
Fabulous straps of grass that stay low, about six inches

Alyssum (*Alyssum* 'Carpet of Snow')
Covered in powder-white blossoms, it drapes over the pot's edge and smells deliciously like a baby

Verbena (*Verbena* x h. 'Romance Silver')
Silvery white blossoms with grey foliage; its long arms grow in, around, and over

Artemisia (*Artemisia stellerana* 'Silver Brocade')
Silver in color, this thick mass of velvet drapes stiffly over the edge of the pot

Violet (*Viola* 'Molly Sanderson')
Wonderful black flower that peeks out here and there

Helichrysum *(Helichrysum petiolare)*
Soft and fuzzy silver foliage

PLANTING SCHEME 5
(a shade container)

Fuchsia (*Fuchsia* 'Other Fellow')
This pale pink fuchsia stands upright in the center

Begonia (*Begonia* 'Non Stop')
Pink, camellialike flowers

White impatiens

Streptocarpela 'Good Hope'
Dangling blue flowers

Nemophila (*Nemophila menziesii* 'Baby Blue Eyes')
Divine sky-blue flowers cascade over pot's edge

Lotus vine *(Lotus berthelotii)*
Fine silver-grey, threadlike leaves

Resources

Previous pages:
The winter view from my back porch.

Antique Pavers
Colonial Brick Company
2222 S. Halsted Street
Chicago, IL 60608
(312) 733-2600
Wholesale only

Architectural Salvage Dealers
Adkins Architectural Antiques
Houston, TX (713) 522-6547

Architectural Antiques
Minneapolis, MN (612) 332-8344

Architectural Artifacts
Chicago, IL (773) 348-0622

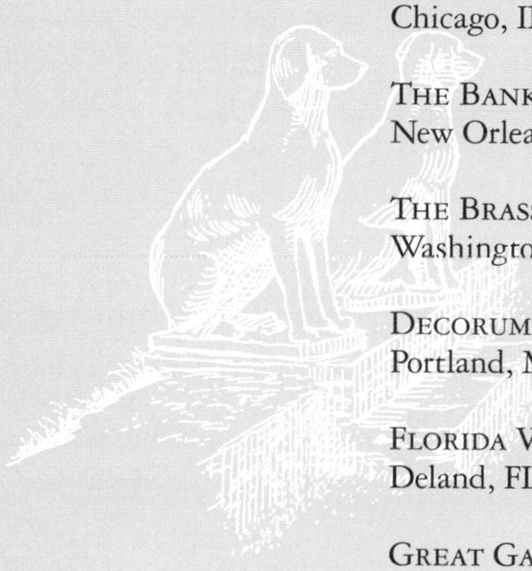

The Bank
New Orleans, LA (504) 523-2702

The Brass Knob
Washington, DC (202) 986-1506

Decorum Hardware
Portland, ME (207) 775-3346

Florida Victorian Architectural Antiques
Deland, FL (904) 734-9300

Great Gatsby's
Atlanta, GA (800) 428-7297

Irreplaceable Artifacts
New York, NY (212) 777-2900

Ohmega Salvage
Berkeley, CA (510) 843-7368

Theatre Architectural Salvage
Kansas City, MO (816) 283-3740

Salvage One
Chicago, IL (312) 725-8243

UNITED HOUSE WRECKING
Stamford, CT (203) 348-5371

BRICKS
CUSHWA BRICK, INC.
P.O. Box 160, 15718 Clear Spring Road
Williamsport, MD 21795
(301) 223-7700
Tumbled and hand-molded bricks

GLEN-GERY BRICK
P.O. Box 207
Iberia, OH 43325
(419) 468-5002
Hand-molded bricks

CONCRETE PIGMENTS AND STAINS
L. M. SCOFIELD COMPANY
6533 Bandini Boulevard
Los Angeles, CA 90047
(800) 800-9900

CP CONCRETE SYSTEMS, LTD.
310 Industrial Avenue
British Columbia V6A 2P3 Canada
(604) 875-9425

CONTAINERS AND ORNAMENTS
TREILLAGE, LTD.
418 East 75th Street
New York, NY 10021
(212) 535-2288

TREILLAGE AT GUMP'S
135 Post Street
San Francisco, CA 94108
(415) 984-9276

THE URBAN GARDENER
1006 W. Armitage Avenue
Chicago, IL 60614
(773) 477-2070

CLASSIC GARDEN ORNAMENTS, LTD.
Longshadow Gardens
R.R. 1, Box 96
Pomona, IL 62975
(800) 634-4429
Manufactures reconstituted limestone in classic, prairie, and rustic designs

NEW ENGLAND GARDEN ORNAMENTS
P.O. Box 431, 38 East Brookfield Road
North Brookfield, MA 01535
(508) 867-4474
Reconstituted sandstone urns, troughs, and ornaments, including sundials

SEIBERT & RICE
P.O. Box 365
Short Hills, NJ 07078
(201) 467-8266
Italian terra-cotta pots

DEROMA USA
245 Fifth Avenue
New York, NY 10016
(212) 725-7953
Wholesale and retail; Italian terra-cotta pots

KINGSLEY-BATE
5587-B Guinea Road
Fairfax, VA 22032
(703) 978-7222
Plantation teakwood boxes

LAKE CREEK GARDEN FEATURES, INC.
P.O. Box 118
Lake City, IA 51449
(712) 464-8924
Lattice pedestals and pyramids

ESPALIER
HENRY LEUTHARDT NURSERIES, INC.
P.O. Box 666, Montauk Highway
East Moriches, NY 11940
(516) 878-1387

FENCES, GATES, AND LATTICE

BAMBOO FENCER
31 Germania Street
Jamaica Plain, MA 02130
(617) 524-6137
Bamboo fences, gates, and arbors

BRATTLE WORKS, INC.
P.O. Box 380536
Cambridge, MA 02238
(617) 864-2110
Architectural lattice; call for a local dealer

EADS FENCE COMPANY
250 E. Kemper Road
Loveland, OH 45140
(513) 677-4040
English hurdle fences; custom lattice, gates and posts, arbors

STEWART IRON WORKS COMPANY (EST. 1886)
P.O. Box 2612, 20 W. 18th Street
Covington, KY 41012
(606) 431-1985
Manufactures new and repairs old ironwork

GARDEN FURNITURE

FLORENTINE CRAFTSMEN
46-24 28th Street
Long Island City, NY 11101
(718) 937-7632

GARDEN ANTIQUARY
2551 Maple Avenue
Courtland Manor, NY 10566
(914) 737-6054

GARDEN CONCEPTS
P.O. Box 241233
Memphis, TN 38124
(901) 756-1649
Furniture, arches, gates, trellises, planters

ROMANCING THE WOODS, INC.
33 Raycliffe Drive
Woodstock, NY 12498
(914) 246-6976
Rustic furniture, fences, and gates

JOHN ROSSELLI INTERNATIONAL
523 Seventy-third Street
New York, NY 10021
(212) 772-2137

MICHAEL D. TRAPP
7 River Road
West Cornwall, CT 06796
(860) 672-6098
Antiques, ornaments, and furniture

MUNDER SKILES
799 Madison Avenue
New York, NY 10021
(212) 717-0150

HISTORIC PICKET FENCE DESIGNS

WALPOLE WOODWORKERS
767 East Street
Walpole, MA 02081
Offers four different historic Williamsburg picket fence designs

Peter Joel Harrison's
FENCES: THE ARCHITECTS AND BUILDERS COMPANION FOR MOST ELEGANT AND USEFUL DESIGNS OF FENCES
$30, available from the author at
2021 Fawndale Drive
Raleigh, NC 27612
(919) 676-0659
Other titles available:
**THE FENCES OF CAPE COD;
BRICKS; GAZEBOS**

BOOKS FOR
YOUR LIBRARY

Adams, James. *Landscaping with Herbs.* Portland, Oregon: Timber Press, 1987.

Arnoux, Jean-Claude. *The Ultimate Water Garden Book.* Newtown, Connecticut: Taunton Press, 1996.

Austin, David. *Old Roses and English Roses.* Wappingers Falls, New York: Antique Collectors Club, 1996.

Austin, David. *Shrub Roses and Climbing Roses.* Wappingers Falls, New York: Antique Collectors Club, 1995.

Barton, Barbara J. *Gardening By Mail: A Source Book.* Boston: Houghton Mifflin, 1994.

Bath, Trevor, and Joy Jones. *The Gardener's Guide to Growing Hardy Geraniums.* Portland, Oregon: Timber Press, 1994.

Boisset, Caroline. *The Garden Sourcebook: A Practical Guide to Planning & Planting.* New York: Crown, 1993.

Bonar, Ann. *The Complete Guide to Conservatory Plants.* North Pomfret, Vermont: Trafalgar Square, 1992.

Bowe, Patrick. *The Complete Kitchen Garden.* New York: Macmillan General Reference, 1996.

Brickell, Christopher, ed. *American Horticultural Society Encyclopedia of Garden Plants.* New York: Macmillan, 1995.

Brookes, John. *The Book of Garden Design.* New York: Macmillan General Reference, 1991.

Brown, George E. *The Pruning of Trees, Shrubs and Conifers.* Portland, Oregon: Timber Press, 1995.

Brown, Jane. *Gardens of a Golden Afternoon: The Story of a Partnership, Edwin Lutyens & Gertrude Jekyll.* New York: Penguin Books, 1994.

Buchanan, Rita, and Roger Holmes, ed. *Taylor's Master Guide to Gardening.* Boston: Houghton Mifflin, 1994.

Buczacki, Stefan. *The Plant Care manual.* New York: Random House, 1993.

Callaway, Dorothy. *World of Magnolias.* Portland, Oregon: Timber Press, 1994.

Clausen, Ruth, and Nicolas Ekstrom. *Perennials for North American Gardens.* New York: Random House, 1989.

Colborn, Nigel. *The Container Garden.* New York: Crescent Books, 1995.

Cowell, F. R. *Garden as a Fine Art: From Antiquity to Modern Times.* Boston: Houghton Mifflin, 1978.

Conder, Susan. *Complete Geranium.* New York: Random House, 1992.

Courtright, Gordon. *Tropicals.* Portland, Oregon: Timber Press, 1995.

Cox, Peter A., and Kenneth N. E. Cox. *Cox's Guide to Choosing Rhododendrons.* Portland, Oregon: Timber Press, 1995.

Crowe, Sylvia. *Garden Design.* New York: Sotheby's Publications, 1994.

De Jong, P. C., H. J. Oterdoom, and D. M. Van Gelderen. *Maples of the World.* Portland, Oregon: Timber Press, 1994.

Denis, John V., and Matthew Kalmenoff. *Complete Guide to Bird Feeding.* New York: Random House, 1994.

Druse, Ken. *The Collector's Garden.* New York: Clarkson Potter, 1996.

Fearnley-Whittingstall, Jane. *Ivies.* New York: Random House, 1992.

Ferguson, Nicola. *Right Plant, Right Place: The Indispensible Guide to the Successful Garden.* Arlington, Texas: Summit Books, 1984.

Fiala, Father John. *Flowering Crabapples: The Genus Malus.* Portland, Oregon: Timber Press, 1995.

Fisher, Sue. *The Hanging Garden: Creative Displays for Every Garden.* North Pomfret, Vermont: Trafalgar Square: 1996.

Fleischmann, Melanie. *American Border Gardens.* New York: Clarkson Potter, 1993.

Flowerdew, Bob. *The Complete Book of Fruit: A Practical Guide to Growing and Using Fruits and Nuts.* New York: Penguin Studio Books, 1996.

Foster, F. Gordon. *Ferns to Know and Grow.* Portland, Oregon: Timber Press, 1984.

Foster, H. Lincoln. *Rock Gardening: A Guide to Growing Alpines and Other Wildflowers in the American Garden.* Portland, Oregon: Timber Press, 1982.

Galle, Fred C. *Azaleas.* Portland, Oregon: Timber Press, 1987.

Gallup, Barbara, and Deborah Reich. *The Complete Book of Topiary.* New York: Workman, 1988.

Goode, Patric, and Michael Lancaster. *The Oxford Companion to Gardens.* Oxford: Oxford University Press, 1991.

Grissell, Eric. *Thyme on My Hands.* Portland, Oregon: Timber Press, 1995.

Heriteau, Jacqueline, and Charles B. Thomas. *Water Gardens: How to Design, Install, Plant, and Maintain a Home Water Garden.* Boston: Houghton Mifflin, 1994.

Hobhouse, Penelope. *Color in Your Garden.* Boston: Little, Brown, 1985.

Hobhouse, Penelope. *On Gardening.* New York: Macmillan General Reference, 1994.

Hobhouse, Penelope. *The Gardens of Europe.* New York: Random House, 1990.

Hobhouse, Penelope. *Penelope Hobhouse's Gardening Through the Ages.* New York: Simon & Schuster. 1993.

Howland, Harris, and Michael Jefferson-Brown. *Gardener's Guide to Growing Lilies.* Portland, Oregon: Timber Press, 1995.

Ketcham, Diana. *Le Desert de Retz.* Cambridge, Massachusetts: MIT Press, 1994.

King, Peter, and Graham Rose. *The 1996 Good Gardens Guide: Over 1,000 of the Best Gardens in the British Isles and Europe.* London: Trafalgar Square, 1996.

Lady Muck (Jane Down). *Magic Muck: The Complete Guide to Compost.* Douglas, Michigan: Pavilion Books, 1994.

Leveque, Georges, and Marie-Francoise Valery. *French Garden Style.* New York: Random House, 1995.

Listri, Massimo, and Cesare M. Cunaccia. *Italian Parks and Gardens.* Milan, Italy: Rizzoli, 1995.

Lloyd, Christopher, and Graham Rice. *Garden Flowers from Seed.* Portland, Oregon: Timber Press, 1994.

Lloyd, Nathaniel. *Garden Craftsmanship in Yew and Box.* Wappingers Falls, New York: Antique Collectors Club, 1995.

Lovejoy, Ann. *The American Mixed Border.* New York: Macmillan, 1993.

Marston, Peter. *The Book of the Conservatory.* North Pomfret, Vermont: Trafalgar Square, 1995.

Mathew, Brian. *The Iris.* Portland, Oregon: Timber Press, 1989.

Matthews, W. H. *Mazes & Labyrinths: Their History & Development.* Mineola, New York: Dover Publications, 1970.

Mawson, Timothy. *The Garden Room: Bringing Nature Indoors.* New York: Clarkson Potter, 1994.

McClure, Susan. *The Herb Gardener: A Guide for All Seasons.* Pownal, Vermont: Garden Way, 1996.

Moody, Mary, ed. *The Illustrated Encyclopedia of Roses.* Portland, Oregon: Timber Press, 1992.

Morse, Harriet K. *Gardening in the Shade.* Portland, Oregon: Timber Press, 1962.

Page, Russell. *The Education of a Gardener.* New York: HarperCollins, 1994.

Phillips, Roger. *Random House Book of Bulbs.* New York: Random House, 1989.

Phillips, Roger, and Martyn Rix. *Random House Book of Perennials.* New York: Random House, 1992.

Plumptre, George. *Collins Book of British Gardens: A Guide to 200 Gardens in England, Scotland and Wales.* London: Collins, 1985.

Recht, Christine, and Max F. Wetterwald. *Bamboos.* Portland, Oregon: Timber Press, 1992.

Richards, John. *Primula.* Portland, Oregon: Timber Press, 1992.

Rose, Graham. *The Classic Garden.* New York: Summit Books, 1992.

Rose, Graham, and Peter King. *The 1996 Good Gardens Guide: Over 1,000 of the Best Gardens in the British Isles and Europe.* London: Trafalgar Square, 1996.

Schmid, W. George. *The Genus Hosta.* Portland, Oregon: Timber Press, 1992.

Stevens, David. *The Garden Design Sourcebook: The Essential Guide to Garden Materials and Structures.* Wappingers Falls, New York: Antique Collectors Club, 1995.

Streatfield, David D. *California Gardens: Creating a New Eden.* New York: Abbeville Press, 1994.

Strong, Roy. *Creating Small Gardens.* New York: Random House, 1987.

Swithinbank, Anne, and Deni Bown (illustrator). *The Sunroom Gardener: A Practical Guide to growing Plants in Sunrooms, Atriums, and Conservatories.* New York: Reader's Digest, 1993.

Tekulsky, Matthew. *Butterfly Garden.* New York: Random House, 1986.

Tenebaum, Frances, ed. *Taylor's Guide to Seashore Gardening.* Boston: Houghton Mifflin, 1996.

Thomas, Graham Stuart. *The Graham Stuart Thomas Rose Book.* Portland, Oregon: Timber Press, 1994.

Turner, Kenneth. *Kenneth Turner's Flower Style: The Art of Floral Design and Decoration.* New York: Grove/Atlantic, 1994.

Vercy, Rosemary. *The Garden in Winter.* Portland, Oregon: Timber Press, 1995.

Verey, Rosemary. *Rosemary Verey's Good Planting Plans.* Boston: Little, Brown, 1993.

Verrier, Suzanne. *Rosa Gallica.* Deer Park, Wisconsin: Capability's Books, 1995.

Verrier, Suzanne. *Rosa Rugosa.* Deer Park, Wisconsin: Capability's Books, 1991.

Wharton, Edith. *Italian Villas & Their Gardens.* New York: Da Capo Press, 1977.

Whiteside, Katherine. *Antique Flowers: A Guide to Using Old-Fashioned Species in Contemporary Gardens.* New York: Random House, 1988.

Wilkinson, Elizabeth, and Marjorie Henderson. *Decorating Eden: A Comprehensive Sourcebook of Classic Garden Details.* San Francisco: Chronicle Books, 1992.

Williams, Robin. *Garden Design: How to Be Your Own Landscape Architect.* New York: Reader's Digest Books, 1995.

Yang, Linda. *The City & Town Gardener: A Handbook for Planting Small Spaces and Containers.* New York: Random House, 1995.

Zabar, Abbie. *The Potted Herb.* New York: Stewart, Tabori & Chang, 1988.

Great Catalogues

Alpen Gardens
173 Lawrence Lane
Kalispell, MT 59901
(406) 257-2540

Andre Viette Farm & Nursery
Rt. 1 Box 16
Fishville, VA 22939

Bluestone Perennials
7211 Middle Ridge Road
Madison, OH 44057
(800) 852-5243

Busse Gardens
13579 Tenth Street NW
Collado, MN 55321

Canyon Creek Nursery
3527 Dry Creek Road
Oroville, CA 95965
(916) 533-2166

Center for Historic Plants
P.O. Box 316
Charlottesville, VA 22902
(804) 984-9860

Complete Garden Clematis Nursery
217 Argilla Road
Ipswich, MA 01938
(508) 356-3197

Cooks Garden
P.O. Box 535
Londonderry, VT 05148

Daffodil Mart
85 Broad Street
Torrington, CT 06790
(800) 255-2862

Fancy Fronds
1911 Fourth Avenue West
Seattle, WA 98119

FOREST FARM
990 Tetherow
Williams, OR 97544
(541) 846-7269

GILBERT WILD & SON
P.O. Box 338
1112 Joplin Street
Sancoxie, MO 64862
(417) 548-3512
Catalog $3.00

HERONSWOOD NURSERY LTD
7530 NE 288th Street
Kingston, WA 98346
(360) 297-4172

IRIS COUNTRY
6219 Topaz Street NE
Brooks, OR 97305
Catalog $2.00

IVIES OF THE WORLD
P.O. Box 408
Weirsdale, FL 32195
Catalog $2.00

J I HUDSTON SEEDSMAN
P.O. Box 1058
Redwood City, CA 94064

JOHNNY'S SELECTED SEEDS
Fross Hill Road
Albion, ME 04910

KLEHM NURSERY
4210 North Duncan Road
Champagne, IL 61821
(800) 553-3715
Catalog $4.00

LAMB NURSERIES
Rt. 1 Box 460B
Long Beach, WA 98631
(206) 642-4856

LOQEE'S GREENHOUSE
141 North Street
Danelson, CT 06239
(203) 774-8038
Catalog $3.00

McCLURE & ZIMMERMAN
108 W. Winnebago
Friesland, WI 53935
(414) 326-4220

OLD HOUSE GARDENS
536 Third Street
Ann Arbor, MI 48103
(313) 995-1486

PINETREE GARDEN SEEDS
Box 300
New Glouchester, ME 04260
(207) 962-3400

PLANT DELIGHTS NURSERY
9241 Sauls Road
Raleigh, NC 27603
(919) 772-4794

PRIMROSE PATH
R.D. 2 Box 110
Scottsdale, PA 15683

ROSES OF YESTERDAY & TODAY
802 Browns Valley Road
Watsonville, CA 95076
Catalog $4.00

SANDY MUSH HERB NURSERY
Rt. 2 Surrett Cove Road
Leicester, NC 28748
(704) 683-2104

SELECT SEEDS
81 Stickney Hill Road
Union, CT 06076
(860) 684-9310

SHEPERD'S GARDEN SEEDS
30 Irene Street
Torrington, CT 06790
(860) 684-9310

SOUTH MEADOW FRUIT GARDENS
10603 Cleveland Ave
Baroda, MI 49101
(616) 422-2411

SUCCULENTA
P.O. Box 480325
Los Angeles, CA 90048
(213) 653-1553

SWAN ISLAND DAHLIAS
P.O. Box 700
Canby, OR 97013
(503) 266-7711
Catalog $3.00

WATERFORD MEADOW
FRUIT GARDENS
10603 Cleveland Ave
Saddle River, NJ 07458
(616) 422-2411

WHITE FLOWER FARM
P.O. Box 50
Litchfield, CT 06759
(860) 496-9600

ENDNOTES

CHAPTER ONE: ONE GARDENER'S JOURNEY
1. *Philip Johnson: The Glass House,* David Whitney and Jeffrey Kipnis, ed. (New York: Pantheon Books, 1993).
2. Wilhelmina F. Jashemski, *The Gardens of Pompeii* (New York: Caratzas Brothers, 1979).

CHAPTER TWO: GETTING STARTED
1. Russell Page, *The Education of a Gardener* (New York: Vintage Books, 1985), p. 110.
2. Alexander Pope, from his *Epistle IV: To Richard Boyle, Earl of Burlington,* 1731, from *Poetry and Prose of Alexander Pope,* Aubrey Williams, ed. (New York: Houghton Mifflin, 1969).
3. John Steinbeck, *East of Eden* (New York: Viking, 1952), p. 29.
4. Thomas Church, *Gardens Are for People* (New York: Reinhold, 1955), p. 43.

CHAPTER THREE: IN SEARCH OF PERSONAL STYLE
1. Remark by Coco Chanel, *Bartlett's Familiar Quotations* (15th edition), Emily Morison Beck, ed. (Boston: Little, Brown, 1980), p. 782.
2. Amy Lowell, "Lilacs," from *The Complete Poetical Works of Amy Lowell* (Boston: Houghton Mifflin [Cambridge Edition], 1955), p. 447.
3. Lester Collins, *Innisfree: An American Garden* (New York: Harry N. Abrams/Sagapress, 1994).
4. Harold Nicolson, "Great Gardens," *New York Times Magazine,* 8/18/63, p. 11.
5. May Sarton, *Plant Dreaming Deep* (New York: W. W. Norton, 1968), p. 121.
6. Edith Wharton, *Italian Villas and Their Gardens* (New York: Century, 1904), p. 5.
7. Sima Eliovson, *The Gardens of Roberto Burle Marx* (New York: Harry N. Abrams/Sagapress, 1991).

CHAPTER FOUR: PUTTING YOUR DREAMS TO WORK
1. *Frank Lloyd Wright Collected Writings* (Vol. I), Bruce Brooks Pfeiffer, ed. (New York: Rizzoli, 1992), p. 220.
2. Thomas Jefferson letter to Charles Willson Peale, 1811, from *The Garden and Farm Books of Thomas Jefferson,* (Golden, CO: Fulcrum, 1987), p. 199.

CHAPTER FIVE: GARDEN WALLS

1. Julia S. Berrall, *The Garden* (London: Thames and Hudson, 1966), p. 30.
2. Robert Frost, "Atmosphere—Inscription for a Garden Wall," from *The Poetry of Robert Frost,* Edward Connery Lathem, ed. (New York: Holt, Rinehart, and Winston, 1969), p. 246.
3. Lawrence Kocher and Howard Dearstyne, *Colonial Williamsburg—Its Buildings and Gardens* (New York: Holt, Rinehart, and Winston, 1976).
4. William C. Mulligan, *The Lattice Gardener* (New York: Macmillan, 1995), p. 79.

CHAPTER SIX: THE GARDEN FLOOR

1. Gelett Burgess, "The Floorless Room," from *The Fireside Book of Humorous Poetry,* William Cole, ed. (New York: Simon & Schuster, 1959).
2. Jan Kowalczewski Whitner, *Stonescaping* (Pownall, VT: Garden Way, 1992).
3. William Morris, "Golden Wings," from *Oxford Book of 19th Century English Verse,* John Hayward, ed. (Oxford, England: At the Clarendon Press, 1964), p. 770.
4. T. S. Eliot, "La Figlia che Piange," from *T. S. Eliot— Collected Poems, 1909–1962* (New York: Harcourt, Brace, Jovanovich, 1963), p. 26.
5. Gertrude Jekyll, from *Wall and Water Gardens* (NH: Ayer, 1983 [originally published in London in 1901 by Country Life]), p. 2.
6. Jens Jensen, from *Jens Jensen: Maker of Natural Parks and Gardens,* by Robert E. Grese (Baltimore: Johns Hopkins University Press, 1992), p. 168.
7. Elizabeth Wilkinson and Marjorie Henderson, *Decorating Eden* (San Francisco: Chronicle Books, 1992).
8. Frances Duncan, *The Joyous Art of Gardening* (New York: Charles Scribner's Sons, 1917), p. 14.

CHAPTER SEVEN: THE ROOF OVERHEAD

1. Robert Penn Warren, "The Place," from *New and Selected Poems, 1923–1985* (New York: Random House, 1985), p. 61.

CHAPTER EIGHT: PASSAGEWAYS

1. Robert Frost, "A Servant to Servants," from *The Poetry of Robert Frost,* p. 64.
2. Alfred Lord Tennyson, "Maud—A Monodrama," from *A Collection of Poems by Alfred Tennyson,* Christopher Ricks, ed. (Garden City, NY: Doubleday, 1972), p. 453.
3. Frances Duncan, *The Joyous Art of Gardening,* p. 22.
4. Alice Morse Earle, *Old Time Gardens* (New York: Macmillan, 1901), p. 387.
5. Francis Bacon, "Of Gardens," from *Essays,* 1625.

CHAPTER NINE: CONTAINERS

1. Madame de Sévigné, 1675, letter to her daughter quoted in Edward Hyams, *A History of Gardens and Gardening* (New York: Praeger, 1971).
2. Hyams, *A History of Gardens and Gardening.*
3. "On the Tuscan Trail: Terra-cotta Unearthed," *Metropolitan Home,* February 1988.

CHAPTER TEN: ORNAMENT

1. Louise Nevelson, *Louise Nevelson: Atmospheres and Environments,* introduction by Edward Albee (New York: Clarkson Potter: 1980 [distributed by Crown in association with the Whitney Museum of American Art]), p. 161.
2. William Lawson, *A New Orchard & Garden,* 1618 (1948 reprint published by Trovillion Private Press, Herrin, IL).
3. William Howard Adams, *French Gardens 1500–1800* (New York: George Braziller, 1979).
4. Vita Sackville-West, *The Illustrated Garden Book, A New Anthology,* Robin Lane Fox, ed., p. 137.
5. Andrew Jackson Downing, *The Theory and Practice of Landscape Gardening,* (New York: C. M. Saxton, Barker, 1860), p. 368.
6. Maria Luisa Gothein, *A History of Garden Art* (Vol. I) (New York: Dutton, 1928), p. 222.
7. John Davis, *Antique Garden Ornament* (Woodbridge, Suffolk, England: Antique Collectors' Club, 1992).
8. William Carlos Williams, "The Red Wheelbarrow," from *The Collected Earlier Poems of William Carlos Williams* (New York: New Directions, 1955), p. 277.
9. T. Geoffrey W. Henslow, *Ye Sundial Booke* (London: W. & G. Foyle, 1935).
10. Amy Lowell, "Behind a Wall," from *The Complete Poetical Works of Amy Lowell,* p. 4.

11. Edward Hyams, *English Cottage Gardens* (Harmondsworth, Middlesex, England: Penguin Books, 1987 [first published by Whittet Books, 1970]), p. 26.

12. Christopher Thacker, *The History of Gardens* (Berkeley: University of California Press, 1979).

13. Nancy Mitford, *Madame de Pompadour* (New York: Harper & Row, 1954).

14. Barbara Gallup and Deborah Reich, *The Complete Book of Topiary* (New York: Workman, 1987).

CHAPTER ELEVEN: FURNITURE

1. Mark Twain in a speech to the New England Society (December 22, 1876), *Bartlett's Familiar Quotations,* p. 622.

2. Julia S. Berrall, *The Garden,* p. 43.

3. Dawn Jacobson, *Chinoiserie* (London: Phaidon Press, 1993), p. 130.

4. Scott Kunst, "Garden-Variety Cast Iron," *Old-House Journal,* January/February 1990 (Vol. 18, no. 1), p. 19

5. Scott Kunst, "Sitting Outside 1865–1940," *Old-House Journal,* July-August, 1993 (Vol. 21, no. 4), p. 22.

CHAPTER TWELVE: INSPIRED PLANTING

1. Mary McCarthy, from *The Stones of Florence* (New York: Harcourt, Brace, 1959).

2. Katherine Mansfield, "The Garden Party," *The Short Stories of Katherine Mansfield* (New York: Knopf, 1970), p. 534.

3. Vita Sackville-West, *In Your Garden* (Marlborough, Wiltshire: Oxenwood Press, 1996), p. 21.

4. Mary McCarthy, *The Stones of Florence,* (1959) p. 114.

5. Andrew Jackson Downing, *The Architecture of Country Houses* (New York: Dover [originally published by D. Appleton in New York, 1850]), p. 208.

6. Frances Duncan, *The Joyous Art of Gardening,* p. 25.

CHAPTER THIRTEEN: THE KITCHEN GARDEN

1. William Lawson, *The Countrie Housewife's Garden,* 1617.

CHAPTER FOURTEEN: MAINTENANCE

1. Jerzy Kosinski, *Being There* (New York: Harcourt, Brace, Jovanovich [Bantam edition], 1971), p. 56.

2. Vita Sackville-West, *The Illustrated Garden Book: A New Anthology,* Robin Lane Fox, ed. (New York: Atheneum), 1986, p. 57.

3. E. B. White, in the introduction to *Onward and Upward in the Garden,* by Katharine S. White (New York: Farrar, Straus, Giroux, 1979), p. xvii.

4. Teijo Ito, *The Japanese Garden* (Tokyo: Zokeisha, 1972).

5. May Sarton, *Plant Dreaming Deep,* p. 127.

CHAPTER FIFTEEN: FIRESIDE GARDENING

1. Anne Bradstreet, from "Meditations Divine and Moral," (1664), *The Works of Anne Bradstreet,* Jeannine Hensley, ed. (Cambridge, MA: Belknap Press of Harvard University Press, 1967), p. 274.

2. Ralph Waldo Emerson, "The Snowstorm," from *The Portable Emerson,* Carl Bode, ed., in collaboration with Malcolm Cowley (New York: Penguin Books [New Edition], 1981), p. 641.

INDEX

PHOTO CREDITS

Ald photo: p. 83.

Amranand, Ping: pp. 10, 18, 36, 51, 57, 84, 93, 116–117, 120, 134 both, 153, 175 right, 184, 199, 201 upper right, 230, 246.

Bardagjy, Paul: p. 216 left.

Bencini, Raffaello: pp. 44–45, 138.

Bibliothèque Nationale, Paris: p. 228.

Bridgeman/Art Resource, NY: p. 65.

Brown, Richard: pp. 152 left, 201 bottom right.

Dagli Orti, Paris: p. 161.

Druse, Ken: pp. 25 upper left, 37, 55, 62, 77 top, 85, 99, 103, 110, 123, 135, 194, 225, 231.

Felber, Richard: pp. 20, 32, 41, 59, 77 bottom right, 89, 95, 132, 142, 148, 158, 163, 169, 172, 216 right, 245.

Gainey, Ryan: p. 54.

Billy Goldsmith . . . Gardens: p. 177 both.

Hales, Mick: Jacket, frontispiece, pp. 25 upper right and bottom right, 31, 46, 48, 66–67, 71, 74, 77 bottom left, 78, 81, 94, 100–101, 114, 118, 125, 130–131, 170 top, 175 left, 176, 188, 192–193, 198, 201 bottom left, 206, 210–211, 214, 226, 238, 240–241, 249.

Hall, John: p. 119.

Harpur, Jerry: p. 195.

Harrison, Peter Joel: p. 75.

Holt, Saxon: pp. 25 bottom left, 104, 126, 129 bottom left and bottom right, 137, 149.

Kane, Dency: pp. 105 left, 129 upper right, 217.

Kunsthistoriches Museum, Vienna: p. 35.

Louvre, D.A.G./© Photo RMN — M. Bellot: p. 187.

Mann, Charles: pp. 72, 90, 201 upper left.

Positive Images/Bussolini, Karen: pp. 146, 181.

Positive Images/Hensel, Margaret: pp. 105 right, 121, 152 right.

Positive Images/Howard, Jerry: p. 97.

Scala/Art Resource, NY: p. 17 top.

Smith, Alex: pp. 166, 244.

Spiegel, Ted: pp. 38, 235.

Stock Image Production/Motte, Vincent: p. 129 upper left.

Stock Image Production/de Virieu, Claire: pp. 252, 266–267.

Talaske, Rick: p. 183.

Taylor, Curtice: pp. 28, 56, 164–165, 170 bottom, 179, 220, 221, 244 top.

Treillage: p. 13.

Uniphoto: pp. 213, 215.

Victoria & Albert Museum (IM 276 and 276A-1913): p. 14.

Williams, Bunny: pp. 145, 154, 155, 234.

Woodyard, Cynthia: p. 237.

About the Authors

Bunny Williams is the president of one of the country's
leading interior design firms, Bunny Williams, Inc.,
and the co-owner of the garden ornament store Treillage,
with branches in New York and in Gump's in San
Francisco. Before founding her own firm she was with
the renowned office of Parish-Hadley for twenty-two years;
she is also a member of the Interior Design Hall of Fame.
A passionate gardener, Bunny maintains a country home
in Falls Village, Connecticut, where she goes whenever
possible to work in her three gardens.

Nancy Drew is a writer who has covered gardening and
interior design for the *Chicago Tribune* for many years.
She is also a contributor to *People, Shape, Self,* and other
publications. She lives in Oak Park, Illinois, with her
husband and two sons.

A Note About the Typography

Garamond is the typeface used for both text and display
type in *On Garden Style.* Modeled on roman type
designs developed by the Venetian printer and publisher
Aldus Manutius, the face was created by Claude Garamond
(1480–1561). The first specimens of Garamond can be
found in books printed in Paris around 1532.